Apostleship Publications

THE
PRAYER OF FAITH

By
LEONARD BOASE, S.J.

Published by the Apostleship of Prayer
at the Messenger Office
1 Spencer Hill, Wimbledon, S.W. 19

De licentia superiorum Ordinis.

Nihil obstat :
      E. LUKE WILLEMS, O.S.B.

Imprimatur :
      H. GIBNEY, *Vic. Gen.*
      Southwarci, die 13 Februarii, 1950.

CONTENTS

Printed for the Apostleship of Prayer *in November 1950*
by the Burleigh Press, *Lewins Mead*, Bristol

FOREWORD

No one, as far as I know, has written a book about walking. Few people, at any rate, will have read such a book if there is one, because walking is so natural and ordinary that we learn how to do it before we learn how to read, and most of us think we know how to do it. But there are books about dancing, because dancing is not as natural as walking. Now the libraries of Christendom are full of books about praying. Does that imply that prayer is not a thing that comes naturally like walking, but an art that has to be specially studied like dancing? Surely it must be as natural to us as breathing or eating, for surely it is the very life of our souls? Yet no one reading even a little way into the books about prayer can help feeling that here is an art, seemingly difficult and artificial; and it would not be too much to say that many are deterred from trying to grow in prayer by this feeling, by the timid conviction that any thing so learned and complicated cannot be for the likes of them. And how, they wonder, can friendship with God be simple and sincere if its growth is governed by rules that make it appear as artificial as ballet-dancing? The heart cannot love to order; friendship is not learnt, as arms-drill is learnt, by numbers; what place have the conventionalities of a book of etiquette in the soul's dealings with its Heavenly Father? Is not the very fragrance of prayer dissipated by the impertinence of a scientific analysis, and do we not run the risk of spiritual posing if we are preoccupied with wondering all the time what state or phase we have reached? Surely, they argue, there must be a difference between Christian prayer, the prayer of sane and normal folk, and those strange contortions of body and twistings of soul that we associate with fakirs, yogis and lamas—or is it llamas? And are not the by-ways of Christian history strewn with the skeletons of those who have lost themselves chasing the dangerous illusions of mysticism?

It is a healthy instinct that thus puts us on our guard. Nevertheless the great Christian library of books on prayer is filled with the works of sages and of saints. There must be some reason for so much work by such great men. If prayer did come to us as naturally as walking, and grow in us with the unerring unconsciousness of our bodily growth, there would be no reason for the books. Yet it must be natural to us, for we need it as much as we need to breathe. What is the explanation?

The explanation is simple : Christian prayer is indeed connatural to man, but it is also supernatural ; it is at once according to his nature and above his nature, and if there are manifold arts which accord with his gifts and yet have to be acquired by training and learning, much more is it true that for fruitful growth and rich development in prayer guidance and assiduous exercise are indispensable. Christian prayer is not merely the development of powers as natural to man as his human powers of knowing and loving; it is also the gradual unfolding and emergence into consciousness of powers different in kind from those of our nature ; it is the opening up of a range and quality of experience utterly

6

beyond the scope of the abilities to know and to love with which we are endowed by nature.

Therefore it seems to me worth while to offer to those who wish to enter into the ways of prayer a book of theory. Many indeed prefer books of practice. They like to be told what to do, without asking why. That is excellent; maybe best. But others find it easier to do what ought to be done if they have some idea of why it is done. Some people ride in motors without even wanting to know what the petrol is for; others cannot enjoy driving till they have taken the engine to bits and put it all back again for themselves. Though this is not a book of theory exclusively, it is offered chiefly to those who like to understand.

And among those, I am envisaging not so much religious, who have abundance of better assistance and guidance, but 'persons living in the world'.

I

THE LIVING WATER

" ONE is good, God," said Our Lord to the young man. He is the only good. He is the source of all goodness : without Him, cut off from Him, everything else withers, grows stale and corrupts. He is the ' dearest freshness deep down things '. Life with its kaleidoscopic fascination may hold us for a while : there are adventurous excitements in simply growing up, in our work, our plans and ambitions, in falling in love, in the building of a home, in the thousand and one interests and allurements that beckon to us ; but they are like a book in a language which we do not understand, brilliantly illuminated with coloured drawings and intricate capitals, rich with the ordered patience of line after line of script ; for a while we can delight in turning over the pages, guessing at the stories from the illuminations, enjoying the beauty of the lettering ; but at length this palls : we want to read the language, to know the meaning. God is the meaning of His creation. It is only because according to its measure it expresses Him, that it has any meaning at all.

There are many who have sensed this. Maybe because sorrow has washed the colour from the illuminations, maybe because disappointment and frustration have torn out some pages and crumpled others, they know that it is not the book of life which in itself can satisfy them. The book is only a message and they seek Him who sent the message. Life for them is faded ; even the tinselly toys of a materialist's paradise on earth have no attraction. How will it help to have more and more luxurious motor cars, faster and faster travel to places that once seemed romantically strange, but are now only the disappointing originals, somewhat washed-out in their colouring, of the photographs in the geographical magazines and the tourist brochures ? What is the use of more and more surprising products of a plastic age, of more and more means of communication ? They want the meaning of it all. They are homesick, dissatisfied, disillusioned. Nothing but God will really meet their need. There is no other living water which can quench this thirst. And prayer is the pitcher that is to be lowered into the well.

Others there are who come seeking the living water in another mood. Life for them is bright ; its colours are gay. They know well that not only the spacious grandeurs of nature but also the manifold amenities of civilisation, the glories of art and all the wonderful works of man, have an abiding value ; but they know this because they know that the true value is the reflected radiance of eternity. From childhood they have known how to read the book ; the universe has never been for them a hostile and terrifying environment, because they have always seen gleaming through it the brightness of God ; they have long ago made the discovery—for them no discovery, but a truth from without beginning —that the world is not only ' charged with the grandeur of God ' but glowing with the manifestation of His tenderness and His love. They seek prayer not in weariness but with eagerness ; they wish to drink deep of that wisdom that does both open their eyes to the unfathomable beauties of the divine and at the same time brighten them to see with ever increasing delight how these beauties are mirrored in the things of time. And for them, as for their wearier companions, prayer is the urn which they must bring to the fountain, the pitcher they must lower into the cool darkness of the well.

II

PRAYER IN GENERAL

FIRST let us say this : the fashioning, moulding, training, the growth of a soul, through infancy, adolescence and maturity, and through the ascending degrees of supernatural development which accompany these stages of growth, all this is a double work, a co-operation, a partnership between God and the soul, a mysterious partnership, beyond the grasp of our intelligence, in which at the same time the activity is all God's and all belongs to the soul. This we can never grasp with our intelligence, unaided, because the activity of God is as much beyond our grasp as His being is, dwelling in light inaccessible. We cannot understand how the work is truly ours and yet all God's, and for the most part we are only aware of it as laboriously and exhaustingly our own. Now the meaning of prayer is in the first place all this work in so far as it is ours ; it is the fashioning of the soul considered from that aspect, that angle, that point of view ; it is all that we do to co-operate with God in His creation and elevation of ourselves. Some day we shall understand that all that is exclusively and completely our very own is the negation and emptiness, the hindrance and limitation which we oppose by sin to the activity of God, all that is " not-prayer ".

But conversely all that is co-operation and partnership, all that is in harmony with God, is prayer in the broad sense of the term. *Laborare est orare* was a monastic axiom ; the monks knew that to work is to pray.

When therefore we become aware of an impulse of the Holy Spirit coaxing us to co-operate with Him by prayer—even such an impulse as may have manifested itself merely through our opening this book—we must not conclude at once that we are being drawn to convert a disused air-raid shelter into an anchor-hold and to summon the Bishop to come and brick up the doorway so that irrevocably we may give ourselves to a life of uninterrupted prayer. Prayer in the first place means all that we do to co-operate with God in the making of our souls.

Thinking of it so, we may liken prayer to a rope. A rope is used for pulling things, such as a temperamental motor car indulging in a fit of the sulks and refusing to proceed to the garage under any power of its own. When you pull a thing by a rope, the pull is exerted through the rope, the rope is what you pull with; and it is the pull that matters; the rope itself—its colour, hairiness and smell for instance—hardly matters at all, except in one respect : its effectiveness and convenience for transmitting the pull.

So it is with prayer. Love is the pull on the rope. It is a matter of secondary importance what the particular activity may be through which we are exerting the pull; the only thing that really counts is the love of God which we achieve through the activity. And ' through ' in the context does not mean ' during '. It is not a question of managing to fit in a number of aspirations between the tickets we punch on the bus, or composing beautiful prayers with one lobe of the brain while we correct school-children's exercise books with the other. There is no harm in fitting in aspirations if you have a gift that way, but it is not what we are talking about at the moment. ' Through ' means that we unite ourselves to God by doing thoroughly with due attention whatever we happen to be occupied in, and doing it with the right intention.

The right intention means that we wish our actions to be in accordance with the will of God, so that they may be to His glory and to our good. It does not mean that we are actually adverting to this idea while doing them, but that the wish has been definitely accepted by our free will, as for instance when we woke up to the fact that baptismal vows were made for us at our baptism and we ratified them and made them fully our own when we so woke up; or, for another instance, when we last said the *Our Father* and meant it.

This raises the question how often ought we to renew this intention. Well, when a young man has fallen in love with a young woman, how often ought he to tell her so? When a couple are happily settled in marriage how often ought they to give expression to the conviction that they are quite pleased to see each other? It is not a question of mathematics. 'Good morning' at breakfast, and 'Good evening' when the breadwinner returns to the little grey home in the west is a reasonable frequency for normal conjugal bliss. But no one would want to ration young Romeo in his protestations of devotion, provided he gets on with his job at the proper time and does not stop weighing out the sugar in order to dispense another sort of sugar. Obviously if there has been a quarrel in the home, or a tiff in the courtship, there is special need for a renewal of 'intention'. And so it is with that intention which transforms our daily activities into prayer; once made, and not revoked, it persists and has its effect. If it is revoked by sin it must be renewed by sorrow for sin. But normally it is not so much an act as a direction. We have set ourselves in motion towards God, and by merely keeping up the motion we are getting nearer the destination. It is not so much a question of renewing the offering of our lives to God as of never doing anything else with them but offer them to Him; not so much turning them to Him as keeping them steadily facing towards Him. And from piety with a pedometer, sanctity with a slide-rule, that spends the time counting and calculating, Good Lord deliver us!

Nevertheless it is a good thing to make our intention explicit, and from time to time to give it expression.

The 'Morning Offering' of the Apostleship of Prayer provides an admirable means of doing so. "O Jesus, through the Immaculate Heart of Mary, I offer Thee the prayers, works, sufferings and joys of this day for all the intentions of Thy divine Heart in the Holy Mass." To make this offering daily is amply enough to ensure that we have the right intention and that in consequence all the actions of our lives are prayer in the broad sense of the term.

This rope of prayer resembles an ordinary piece of rope in this : it is made up of strands, woven or twisted together. The first strand of the rope is work, the ordinary daily job, what we do because we have to do it, not because we like it (though there is no reason why we should not like it ; it is work even if we do), our duty, the way we earn our living. This is capable of being made a part of our prayer ; through it we can love God and the growth of our soul can be assisted. And it becomes prayer, as we have explained, not by reason of the attention which we pay to God during it but by reason of the intention with which we do it.

The second strand of the rope is play. Play means everything that we do because we like it, not because we have to ; everything that we do for recreation, for amusement, as a hobby, as an interest. This too can become part of our prayer. Needless to say, play is the point at which we are most likely to be exposed to temptation, and nothing can unite us to God which is sinful. More than a drowsy watchfulness may be necessary to make sure that our ' play ' is fit to be offered to God ; but this in itself will be a safeguard keeping us from sin. What we should take much care to avoid is that cramping heritage of the Puritan heresy, that often unconscious presupposition that because a thing is pleasant it can at best be only something that does not hinder us from reaching God, but cannot be a means that positively helps us to do so.

The third strand of the rope we might call the Cross.

14

The Cross, which as Our Lord told us every man must take up daily if he wishes to follow Him, means more especially all that goes athwart, against, across our inclinations, our likes and dislikes, our choices and aversions. The prayer which forms the third strand of the rope consists in that submission of the will to God by which we say, not perhaps in words but in the practical language of actions, " Thy will be done ". Everything, from a shattering tragedy that robs us of all that we hold dearest, down to a bus that passes us by when we signal it, is part of the Cross. At each succeeding moment of our lives we are held in a matrix of circumstances, and that matrix is at that moment for us the Will of God. To respond with loyal acceptance of God's Will is prayer in one of its richest forms. And we should remember that this acceptance is not confined to those things which go counter to our desires ; Our Lord spoke of them more especially because it is in them that we find difficulty in submitting to God's will ; but none the less included in this strand of prayer are all the pleasant agreeable things ; to accept God's will in gratitude with delight is none the less to accept it. Our Lord bids us pray " Thy will be done on earth as it is in heaven ", and in heaven there are no hardships to accept, God's will is all our joy.

Now there is a fourth strand of the rope of prayer. It is that to which we give the name of prayer, in the more exact and special sense. It is in fact the subject of this book. What is it ? To give the answer in a phrase, it is loving God through some sort of know-ledge, awareness, attention, which is directed to Him, loving Him through thinking about Him. And you will see at once that this corresponds to what we have in mind when in ordinary human relationships we think of love. The question ' Do you love me ? ' expects for its answer precisely this, that the one whose love is sought should have the seeker constantly in mind, and through some sort of knowledge, awareness or attention should arouse in the heart just what we mean by love. You will see also that this corresponds exactly to the definition in the catechism : prayer is the raising up of the mind and heart to God.

Briefly, then, there are two ways in which we do our share in the work of developing our spiritual life, that work which is a partnership between God and ourselves : one is the way of action; in this way we achieve love of God by responding to Our Lord's appeal " If you love Me keep my commandments "; this is prayer in one deep sense of the word, and we have summed it up under the image of the first three strands of the rope ; it is relatively outward or exterior. The other is inward or interior ; it is concerned with our awareness of God, with our consciousness in so far as that consciousness is turned towards God, with our thoughts, our mind-life, our attention, in their bearing upon God. This is the fourth strand of the rope. Clearly it can be closely intertwined with the others, for it is often possible to be aware of God while we are doing things for Him. The fourth strand is evidently the most precious of all, for to love God by turning towards Him the noblest of our faculties, the faculty of knowing, is evidently the highest of our achievements ; contemplation is the final end for which we were created. Nevertheless we must not be led by our realisation of this truth into thinking that the value in God's eyes of the other things that we do in His service is measured by the degree of attention to Him which we can succeed in combining with those other things. The worth of those things in His eyes depends not on this factor of attention, but on the intention, by which our deeds are dedicated to Him. Many of them demand of us concentrated attention, and to divide our attention would be to do them badly. We love God by keeping His commandments, by living and acting in such a manner as redounds to His glory, being in relation to Him as a masterpiece to the poet or artist who made it. The intention, broadly understood as the will to serve and love the Divine Goodness, is what gives essential worth to our lives and makes them prayers of action. If indeed we can add to this a conscious communion of spirit with God, if our actions are illumined from within by the light of our awareness of Him, they are still more precious in His eyes, and still more splendid is the masterpiece wrought by the divine Artist in His gracious and reverent co-operation with ourselves, who are at once His work and His partners in the work. This awareness, this attention, this lifting of the mind and heart to God, is prayer in the more exact and special sense of the word; this is the fourth strand of the rope.

Now we should notice this: there are some things we do which we should not hesitate to call prayer, such as being present at Mass, receiving the sacraments, reciting prayers or joining in the singing of hymns. Are these precisely the fourth strand of the rope? Not precisely. They are in the first place actions, and they might be classed as forming part of the first strand, work or duty. It is indeed right and proper that while we are doing them we should turn our attention to God; the Catechism warns us that those who at their prayers think neither of God nor of what they say do not pray well, but offend God if their distractions are wilful. Nevertheless they do not offend God if their distractions are not wilful. In other words, these actions—walking in a procession, for example—have their first value from the intention which governs them, and if through human frailty attention fails, that first value remains. These things are not precisely what we are speaking of when we speak of the fourth strand of prayer, the raising of the mind and heart to God. They are normal and easy instruments by which we attain to that raising of the mind and heart, but they are not identical with it; a railway train is a normal and easy instrument by which we make a journey, but the train is not identical with the journey. These actions, such as being present in

17   B

church during Mass, have a value apart from the attention to God which we may succeed in achieving during them; they are first of all actions which are worship of God, even should we fail to make our consciousness correspond completely with them while we are doing them; the duty of going to Mass on Sunday is fulfilled even by one for whom the whole time is spent in a losing battle with distractions; a Master of Ceremonies, for example, hears Mass even though a great deal of his attention is absorbed in seeing to it that the ceremony is duly and correctly performed. But when we speak of the fourth strand of prayer we are speaking precisely of the interior element of attention of the focusing of consciousness on God, of steeping our awareness in the great fact that He exists, that we are in Him, that in Him we live and move and have our being. It is with prayer in this more exact sense that this book is chiefly concerned.

A life of prayer is a growth, like any other life but God's. A growth has stages or phases. The phases of the life of prayer are distinguishable from each other chiefly because of changes in this interior element of which we are speaking, and more exactly or more discernibly in the element or factor which consists in knowledge or consciousness. The other element or factor is love. It is not so easy to discern or to describe changes or phases in this; there is in a healthy and fruitful life of prayer a steady development of strength in love, and there is a noticeable change perceived in the dwindling away of the emotions or affections that are an accompaniment of love in its beginnings. But on the whole it is chiefly by the changes in the factor of knowledge that the phases of prayer can be distinguished. It is as if the rope of prayer were a line flung from a ship when mooring at the quayside: first a light line is flung and then a stouter hawser is drawn by the light line, but the pull or tension remains the same in kind, only increasing in strength; in fact it is in order to allow of greater strength in the pulling that the quality of the rope is changed. So in prayer the love remains constant, only increasing in strength, and it is to bear the greater tension of growing love, and the growing trials with which God tests it, that the quality of the factor of knowledge is changed.

This book therefore is concerned chiefly with the growth and development of our awareness of God, and its central point—to repeat a remark made in the foreword—is that the outline of a normal development in prayer is the gradual emergence into consciousness of supernatural powers implanted in the soul at baptism and intended to reach their full fruition in the Beatific Vision, the face-to-face knowledge of the incomprehensible Beauty, Truth and Goodness Who is God.

III

THE BECHER'S BROOK

THERE is a Becher's Brook in the steeplechase of prayer, where the field is frequently thinned out. There are Goodwin Sands in this Channel, 'a very dangerous flat and fatal, where the carcass of many a good ship lies buried'. There is a desert on this Golden Journey, where nearly everyone wanders lost and parched, and some die of thirst. And it is at this commonest of difficulties that it seems to me best to begin.

My reason is this : people who pick up books about prayer are not likely to be strictly beginners in prayer. One does not begin anything with a book. Whether it be cricket, or drawing, or science, or music, the beginning is made by doing, not by reading, or at least with a living teacher not with the dried lessons of print. And above all the beginnings of prayer are made that way. Nowadays especially, when retreats are an established part of Catholic life, it is a remote improbability that anyone who feels a desire to deepen the interior life, strong enough to lead to the reading of such a book as this, will not be already familiar with the beginnings. For completeness' sake those beginnings will be dealt with, but later, when for those already versed in them a new light may perhaps be thrown upon them by the discussion of this common difficulty of which we are now speaking ; while even for others, to whom simple instruction in methods of mental prayer would be useful because not previously received, such instruction will be all the more intelligible in the light of that discussion.

To whom, then, are these pages primarily addressed ? To such as are seeking God in prayer and feel within themselves an impulse or a need to grow in mental prayer ; to such therefore as have some knowledge of what mental prayer is and are prepared to devote some constant part of their time to it. It may not be a great part ; it may be only a quarter of an hour saved at much cost from the devouring exigencies of a busy day. It may be more. Many who seek this closer union of consciousness with God have dedicated themselves entirely to his service, and living the life that is technically known as " Religious ", reap the reward of their sacrifice by having an hour or more in the day preserved for this. But whether it be long or short, it is vital that the giving of time to prayer should be constant. The teaching of St. Francis de Sales has borne fruit, and nowadays it is being realised with increasing clearness that holiness is not a specialised career for those who enter the cloister ; but if anyone thinks that such holiness as St. Francis preached to ' persons living in the world ' can be attained without the constant practice of interior prayer—then at any rate this is no book for such a one.

To all who persevere in mental prayer—the statement can be made with confidence—to all there comes sooner or later that darkness and sense of failure and frustration which is our selected starting-point. Until the clue to the maze is found, there will be pain and distress, even perhaps discouragement and despair for those who find themselves lost in the maze, and even for those whose path is still straight and sunlit there should be no harm in having the clue before it is needed. The clue lies in the statement which is the key-note of what we are saying : that the normal history of a life of prayer is the gradual emergence into consciousness of a supernatural mode of knowledge. It is in order to emphasise this point, as well as because it is the encountering of this darkness which often enough first sends people looking for books on prayer, that I have decided to begin here.

But before we face the difficulty itself, what in general terms is mental prayer ? It is simply trying to love God by thinking about Him. Ordinary prayer, vocal prayer means that we try to turn our attention to God by using forms of words which guide our thoughts to Him. Mental prayer means that without adverting to the words in which our thoughts are clothed, we try to fix our attention on truths that concern God, either by dwelling on the life of Our Lord, or by considering the teaching of the Church, or by using some series of thoughts and reflections prepared for us and printed in a book with some such title as ' Meditations ', or in some similar way. The immediate purpose of meditation or mental prayer is to educate and nourish the mind. We meditate with the mind, or intellect, or intelligence, or reasoning power —there are several names for the same thing. It is through this mental activity that we exert the pull of love, and usually we try to emphasise this by endeavouring to make the intellect kindle the heart, and to conclude the meditation by acts of love, transforming what might have been abstract and impersonal into something real and personal. But the immediate purpose or objective is the training and formation of the mind towards an increasingly habitual realisation of the great fact that God exists.

Such is meditation in brief. There have been elaborated various methods and systems to help us to achieve it. Of those presently. Such is meditation, and perhaps for a time, maybe for a long time, it succeeds. Then comes the darkness.

I do not mean that there may not have been ups-and-downs, periods of facility alternating with periods of darkness, times of depression and times of brightness, stretches of enthusiastic endeavour contrasting with listless seasons of waning eagerness, before the darkness settles down. It is the normal thing that such a law of up-and-down should rule even during a time when broadly speaking meditation is the accustomed and desired form of our mental prayer.

Nor do I mean that the relatively permanent darkness comes suddenly, or is suddenly perceived. We have to speak of these phases as if they were sharply outlined. In practice they are rarely so.

> " For note, when evening shuts,
>   A certain moment cuts
>   The deed off, calls the glory from the grey,"

said Browning; but it would be a very alert observer who could press a stop-watch precisely at the ' certain moment '.

As often as not, I would say, it is after a period of waning eagerness, when absorbed in some fresh and interesting activity we have given up the habit of meditation, or if bound to it by duty have done it perfunctorily, that we come to our senses so to speak, aroused perhaps by a retreat or some similar event, and find ourselves lost, irretrievably it seems, in the desert. No efforts, however frantic, seem to be of any avail. Not only do we feel no taste for prayer, but even if spurred by an uneasy conscience we over-ride the distaste, we have apparently lost the knack. Try as we may it appears impossible to fix the attention on any thought, however carefully chosen and prepared; or if we succeed for an instant, imperceptibly the focus of attention slips at once to some irrelevant side-issue, or to some completely unconnected thought. The time of prayer becomes like a tiresome dream, one of those dreams in which we are always just going to see or hear something that we are curious about, some unknown thing which persistently attracts us, and as tantalisingly eludes us, so that we never reach it but wake vaguely dissatisfied. Or prayer becomes like a state of fatigue in which a name is on the tip of the tongue, or a fact just peeping round the corner, and we cannot say the name or recall the fact. Needless to say there is no emotional pleasure in this prayer, for there appears to be no love of any sort. It seems quite impossible to transform the intellectual discussion (which anyway isn't there) into a personal colloquy with God, and if there is one thing which is clearer than another it is that there does not seem to be any God to hold a colloquy with. All is dark, dry, cold. The only difference between this and the state of careless neglect which perhaps preceded it, is the gnawing discomfort which makes us keep to the time of prayer, partly for fear of missing the return of the old facility, partly from an obscure realisation that for all its intolerable boredom, this prayer, when we rise from it, has somehow given us a satisfaction that is not merely the sense of duty faithfully done, and a strength which we cannot feel but which we know we can rely on in facing the daily realities.

But we are fortunate if we perceive even this gnawing discomfort. This state in prayer is the Becher's Brook ; this is where many a gallant jumper takes a fall, and alas ! where many jockeys fail to mount again. This is the desert where all wander for a time and many die.

What is the meaning of it all ? Briefly this : that in order to stimulate the development of a supernatural mode of knowledge, the Holy Spirit, Master of Prayer, employing to a large extent the operation of quite normal secondary causes, puts the natural powers of thinking into a state of abeyance, or in more homely phrase sends the mind to the nursery to sleep.

It should of course be noticed that not all distaste for

23

prayer or difficulty in it is due to this action of the Holy Spirit. Such distress may be due to blunting the spiritual taste by over-indulgence in unspiritual tastes. But that kind is different : you just dislike praying and find it an irksome duty ; whereas when the Holy Spirit is using dryness to advance a soul's prayer there is a great longing to pray underlying all the difficulty and the boredom.

We can sometimes be reassured that our dryness in prayer is part of the process of growth by a curious and perhaps puzzling phenomenon. It is that when before the time of prayer we are preparing matter for prayer, we find it extraordinarily easy to think ; whole rivers of thought suggest themselves ; with eager optimism we assure ourselves that next time at least we shall be able to meditate. The next time comes, and down comes the curtain. Not a thought recurs. Even if by reading the very matter which was so luminous while we were making preparation, we try to recapture the vistas of thought, it is useless. A marked contrast like this suggests that the Holy Spirit is employing something more than the operation of normal secondary causes.

What then is it that He is seeking to stimulate ? What is the supernatural power whose emergence requires such birth-pangs ? For answer we must begin by considering the question " What is Faith ? ".

IV

FAITH

IF we are eye-witnesses of an event we know that it has taken place ; we do not just believe—we know. Similarly we know truths when we have proved them to our satisfaction, by logical steps from secure foundations ; we do not believe—we know. But if we are told something by a trustworthy person, then we believe it ; to believe is to accept a truth on the word of another.

That is faith. Divine faith is believing what God says because He says it; this is an act of divine faith. The power of doing so, the ability to believe, is the virtue of faith.

Now one of the most surprising assertions with which the Catholic Church meets an inquirer or would-be convert is the assertion that without the aid of a gift beyond the scope or range of human powers the intending convert will not be able to believe the things that God says, on the strength of His word. It is an assertion that would surprise even cradle-Catholics were it not so familiar to them as to pass unnoticed. You cannot accept God's revelation unless God gives you a supernatural gift called the grace of faith. " Faith is a supernatural gift of God which enables us to believe without doubting whatever God has revealed." The idea is quite familiar to Catholics and most probably it is only on encountering a friend who says " I would like to believe as you do but I can't " that a Catholic first realises that there is anything supernatural about an act of faith. In itself, to those brought up in Catholicism, the act of believing what God says, because He says it, appears as easy and natural as believing a policeman when you ask him the time and he tells you. It seems just the same, because it employs the same mental machinery; yet we know from God's revelation, through the Church, that it lifts the machinery on to a higher plane of achievement, and that without this lift-up, which is the grace of faith, our mental apparatus would not produce the result of accepting God's word as true.

That such supernatural help is needed, and is supplied may be more evident to us when we consider the things which it enables us to believe. They are things which the unbeliever scouts as incredible or impossible. They are what we call mysteries, truths which are beyond the grasp of reason but revealed by God. It is fairly easy to realise that in order to accept these mysteries as objectively true we need God's help. We are tempted

25

at times to agree with the small boy's definition " Faith is a supernatural gift by which we believe without doubting things which we know are not true ". And in our effective idea of what the gift of faith is we are inclined to stop there, to think of it as being only a help to believe what we find it difficult to believe. In everyday life, in which by far the greater part of what we think we know for certain does in point of fact come to us by natural faith in the trustworthiness of others—experts not excluded—there is a rough-and-ready check on our acceptance of statements. We apply a double check : we weigh the intrinsic probability or possibility of the statement against our estimate of the reliability of the speaker, and if the improbability or impossibility does not outweigh the credit that the speaker enjoys with us, we accept the statement as true. When it is a question of believing God we judge that His credit, His trust-worthiness, is unlimited ; but even so, the mysteries of His revelation being at first glance so contrary to our ideas of what is possible or probable, we experience a sort of shock ; we find ourselves faced with a difficulty. Then it is that we realise that believing a person is one way of doing him honour, and therefore unhesitatingly to accept God's declarations on the strength of His infinite truthfulness is one way to worship Him, and consequently we have the good will to believe ; and then it is that God gives us the gift of faith enabling our minds to accept as true declarations for which we can see no reason except His making of them, and against which reason itself offers strong objections. It is for instance contrary to all our experience that the same thing should be in several places at once ; reason, based on experience, therefore suggests strong objection to believing that the Body and Blood of Christ are present in every consecrated Host at once. This objection the gift of faith dissolves.

But that is not all that the gift of faith does. The central point of what we are trying to say about prayer rests on this : that the gift of faith is a supernatural addition to, or extension of, our human powers of knowing, the first effect of the gift being what has just been said, namely that it enables us to accept as true statements made in the revelation of God, and the further effect being to enable us to know—to use the power of knowledge—in a manner which that power of knowledge cannot attain when left to its natural range or scope. This is the point we are trying to emphasise. God has by the gift of faith implanted in us a power of knowing which exceeds the natural human powers of knowing; 'implanted' is not quite the right word; 'grafted on' would be better, because the supernatural power of faith is something added to the power of knowing which is in us as men already. It is this which the Holy Spirit is endeavouring to stimulate when He plunges us into that darkness of which we have been speaking. It is as if the power of knowing in us were like a carpet, and the focus of our attention or conscious-ness were like the beam of a pocket-torch shining on the carpet immediately before our feet; the Holy Spirit then lifts the torch a little, causing it to shine on the path some distance ahead, and therefore leaving in darkness the part around our feet that previously had been lit up; the beam going further off appears to us fainter; that is, our attention, taken away from the meditation to which we had been accustomed, leaves our thoughts in seeming darkness, and because we have not readjusted ourselves to the change, we feel that we are doing nothing and are wasting our time.

But what is it that this new power of faith should enable us to " see ", and what does " seeing " mean in the circumstances ?

Briefly, God. Only, in the circumstances " seeing " does not mean finding out anything about God that we did not know before. It means simply an awareness of the reality, the fact, the presence, of God, different in kind from the sort of awareness of God which we would have, if by a process of reasoning we had satisfied our minds that He does exist; different, because 'experimental' or 'experienced'; different because supernatural. This is the immediate goal of that darkness and emptiness which causes so many to think that their prayer is failing; it is to concentrate attention, to focus consciousness, upon an awareness of the presence of God, which, just because it is supernatural, might be masked by the nearer and relatively brighter light of our ordinary knowledge; just as the light of bright but distant stars is rendered invisible by the nearer and relatively brighter light of the moon, and to see the further stars we must have a moonless night.

Prayer, we said, in the special sense of loving God through some sort of thinking or awareness of Him, is the fourth strand of the rope. Looking closer, we find that this fourth strand is rather like a length of flex, or electric wire. Flex appears to us to consist of soft, cloth-like material; but examination of it shows that this is only a covering; inside the covering is a metal wire; it is this metal wire which carries the current. So it is with the fourth strand of prayer: at first it appears to consist of thoughts, ideas, imaginative pictures, all of which are just like our ordinary everyday mental activity, because they are in fact the activity of our natural mental powers. But, though perhaps unrealised at first, unperceived, Christian prayer, even from its beginnings, has a core which is supernatural. The core is faith. Without this grace of faith, we could not, as St. Paul tells us, even say that Jesus is Lord.[1] The normal aim of the Christian interior life is to live by faith, that is to deepen and strengthen our faith, making it more and more the driving-force of our lives—in union of course with charity, for a faith not vitalised by love would be a piece of dead wire. In our ordinary relationships with the world around us, this endeavour is shown by our acting according to the mind of Our Lord, trying to understand things from His point of view, taking His standard of values for our standard, making

28

His desires our desires, and in general having our religion as the effective map and compass which guides our life. And in prayer, in mental prayer, we begin by simply spending the time trying by concentrated attention to shape our minds to this pattern, for " yours is to be the same mind which Christ Jesus showed ".[2] While this is our principal occupation—in prayer, and of course implicitly out of the time of prayer also—we are not likely to be noticeably conscious of the specially supernatural element which is developing in the texture of our thoughts. The growth of it is gradual, imperceptible. A convert, returning on a visit to non-Catholic relatives some time after conversion, may sometimes be able to notice, by contrast with the mentality of those relatives, this growth or change ; but as a rule it is too gradual, too subtle also, to be observed. From time to time, during mental prayer in this mind-shaping period, there may be moments when the presence of God is more vividly felt. But as in such a period these moments of " consolation " are usually accompanied by warmth of emotional feeling, by " sweetness " similar to the sweet delight of ordinary human love, it is likely that attention will be drawn rather to this emotional accompaniment than to the obscure supernatural awareness of the presence of God.

Now it is the aim of the Holy Spirit to develop the virtue of faith in us. Therefore, when we are sufficiently trained in that habit of mind which makes the teaching of Christ and our loyalty to Him an effectual force in our daily life, the Holy Spirit usually leads us into this night of darkness of which we have been speaking. He hides the moon of intelligible thoughts about God and about Christ Our Lord in order that we may begin to look for the far stars of immediate supernatural awareness of His presence. He takes away emotional sweetness from our consolation lest that, too, excellent thing though it is, should distract us from the immeasurably more excellent tasting of the divine reality. The covering begins to be stripped off the flex; we find that the fourth strand of prayer has become in our hand a naked piece of wire; prayer is reduced to being nothing but a dogged reassertion of faith, accompanied by a dry, unemotional, and seemingly unreal will to love God, which appears to us very different from what we thought was love, even more so in fact than dehydrated eggs differ from real shell-egg out of the nest. This is the crucial point in the normal life of prayer. This is the jump that thins the field. To be able to give at this time confidence and reassurance, is one of the most valuable things a director or adviser can do. I am trying to do it here by trying to help people to understand what is happening when this darkness comes in prayer.

It is not darkness, really; it is not emptiness absolutely. It is a relative darkness, a comparative emptiness. It is the " night of sense " (for St. John of the Cross includes intellect also when he speaks of " sense ").[3] It is the preparation for, and the beginning of, a new way of reaching God.

Faith is a supernatural gift of God which begins by aiding the natural power of " sense " to accept on God's assurance mysteries, stated in human language, whose " what " and whose " how " are beyond the grasp of " sense "; but faith is also radically the power which, when it has passed through its adolescence here on earth, where it is the *lumen fidei* (the light of faith), will be transformed into the *lumen gloriae*, that light of face-to-face knowledge of God which we call the Beatific Vision. Our life on earth, our *via*, is the adolescence of this knowledge, the virtue of faith, grafted at baptism on to our human powers of knowledge, is designed to develop into the Gifts of the Holy Ghost which are the perfection and flowering of the virtue, and in particular the Gifts of Understanding and Wisdom; we may think of Understanding as that effect of faith which enables us to see created reality in the light of God, seeing Him in all things and seeing all in Him, perceiving that meaning which alone gives value to the beautiful lettering and fascinating illustrations of the Book which is the world; and we may think of Wisdom as being that further effect of faith which enables us, though dimly, ' as in a glass darkly ', to turn the dazzled eyes of our consciousness towards the source of all light, towards the unbearable beauty, the inaccessible exaltation of Him Who is.

But almost at the outset of the path that leads this way there is a desert, a dry land. For many, it would seem, the path runs for a long time through this dry waste. Here there is need of courage, and because this need appears so great I have chosen to set first in this explanation of prayer a reassurance that all is well, and that seeming failure in prayer is usually the surest augury of success. Now let us turn back and consider again the meaning of what we call meditation or mental prayer.

V

MENTAL PRAYER

PRAYER, in the special sense we are now discussing, means loving God through some sort of attention or thought. The purpose of meditation or mental prayer is to fill the mind with thoughts suitable for this purpose. It is to train the mind, to form a mentality. The mentality aimed at is that which is an apt receptacle for that " understanding " which sees God in all things and all things in God; it is the habit of mind which is God-conscious; it is that bent or inclination on account of which attention will, by a sort of second-nature, swing round again to God, as the compass-needle swings to the magnetic north, the moment it is freed from the attraction of other thoughts.

The thoughts and ideas which we endeavour to form in our minds in mental prayer are in brief the revelation made by Christ, together with whatever may help our understanding of this revelation. To find suitable matter for meditation we turn therefore principally to the life of Our Lord in the Gospel, to the teaching of the Church, and to that full-stored granary of spiritual writings which is our inheritance; we also turn to living teachers, speaking to us in sermons and conferences.

Hence mental prayer, as regards the element of knowledge which is an essential part of it, is very like education; in fact it *is* education, in practical religion.

Nevertheless it differs from education, as the act of pulling a barge with a tow-rope differs from the tow-rope. Prayer is only truly prayer, in the special sense, when there is a pull on the rope, when we are loving God through the thoughts. Hence it is not the same thing as study or education; even study of theology can remain mere study and not become prayer in the sense in which we are here speaking of prayer; it remains that when it is a mere intellectual exercise and is not a channel of thoughts through which our love goes to God. But it should be remembered that even study, whether it is the study of divine things or not, can become prayer in the other sense of the term, if it is an action done for the glory of God and offered to Him by a right intention.

There are therefore two separate things to master if we are to achieve meditation or mental prayer. One is concerned with getting the right thoughts into our mind; the other is concerned with making those thoughts the means of loving God, the ladder by which our love is lifted up to God.

In practice, at the beginning of a life of prayer, the second of these two aims is achieved principally outside the time of prayer; it is achieved in conduct in daily life; we meditate in order to make ourselves better able to give to God that solid kind of love which Our Lord asked for when He said 'If you love Me keep My commandments'. The instant testing of an idea by action has been called the prince of faculties. If we want to be sure that our thoughts of God are really lifting us up to love of Him, it is chiefly by their effect on our daily life that we must test them. Hence it is that in the early stages of mental prayer it is an invaluable practice to put before ourselves, as we embark on that river of thoughts which we hope the meditation will prove to be, a definite objective engaging the will, such as an explicit resolution to mould our conduct in a certain way.

Meditation also aims at making thought the means of loving God in yet another manner. When we speak of love we ordinarily have in view a state of mind in which emotion plays a part, tender affectionate emotion which is at once an index of, and an aid to, the desire in the will that is the essence of love. Meditation aims at evoking in us such a state of mind. One practical means of doing this is so to order our thoughts that they bring us into direct personal awareness of Our Lord, or of Our Father, or of the Spirit who is their Love. And we can do this by the simple, obvious method of addressing the Divine Persons in words, or concluding our meditation with a colloquy. A colloquy is merely a conversation, talking with someone. It may also be a help to address in the same way Our Lady or the angels and saints. Emotion so aroused is not only a joy to ourselves but also an aid to conduct. We shall keep Our Lord's commandments all the better for having felt the thrill of affection for Him. Such an aid might be called a lubricant. We have to remember that lubricant is meant for oiling the works, not for drinking. To make that pleasure which we feel when our thoughts have kindled in us the warmth of affection the aim and objective of prayer, is spiritual gluttony. We must constantly test ourselves by the other effect of meditation, its influence on our conduct outside the time of prayer to make sure that we are not seeking this pleasure in a selfish way.

C

The other thing to be mastered if we are to achieve meditation is concerned with getting the right thoughts into our mind, thoughts that will be a suitable means for loving God. One way to do this is to live continuously in an atmosphere that tends to suggest such thoughts, to eliminate from our lives as far as possible everything that jars and is out of harmony with this aim, to build a wall to keep the world outside. This was what the monks of old sought to do, and what contemplative religious still seek to achieve. The cloister is meant to keep out as far as possible all that would disturb and trouble the soul and force into the mind distracting concerns. But the cloister is pre-eminently for a chosen few, called to a severe life of atoning hardship, and perhaps endowed with special graces of prayer.

The majority, even of religious—and by ' religious ' we mean men and women living under the three vows of poverty, chastity and obedience, living as members of some congregation or order—the majority live to-day a life that is not cloistered in that sense. They aim at the ' mixed ' life, which seeks to combine prayer with exterior activity. And ' persons living in the world ', to whom St. Francis de Sales more particularly addressed his preaching, have perforce to find prayer in the mixed life if they are to find it at all. It was for such as these that St. Ignatius Loyola in the Spiritual Exercises elaborated the methodic approach to prayer : he was dealing precisely with this problem, the problem how to get the right thoughts into the mind. To express it shortly he adopted an idea that even before his time was becoming common ; an idea which the Dominicans had introduced into their own practice as early as the Chapter of Milan, 1505, and which the Franciscans also adopted,[4] the idea of systematic, regular mental prayer —a time fixed each day, to be devoted exclusively to mental prayer and nothing else, not even the liturgical office. This seems to us now something so familiar that it is difficult to realise that it was not at first a matter of rule for monks and nuns. The explanation of this we have given : it was not felt necessary to add a time of obligatory mental prayer to the existing obligations of the chant and the liturgy, simply because the whole of the rest of the time was designed to be something very close to mental prayer, and the monks were free to give as much time as they wished, out of their leisure, to contemplation. But the Dominicans, whose vocation as preachers necessarily involved them in the tumult of life outside the cloister, and the Franciscans, who were to knead the leaven of Christ into the world, came to see the need for methodic training of the mind for prayer. And St. Ignatius, through the instrument of the Exercises, offered precisely this training not only to his own followers, who were designed for a life of distracting activity, but to all who wished to take it. Let us examine the idea of meditation more especially with regard to the factor of thinking that enters into it.

The situation we assume is this : you wish to pray ; to deepen and enrich your interior life, to reach a habitual union of mind and heart with God ; perhaps you have entered a religious congregation and meditation is one of your duties ; perhaps your vocation is in the world, but you have made up your mind that what Quakers and others can do, you can do, and you are going to set aside some portion of the day for mental prayer, if it is only a quarter of an hour last thing at night. You feel that to spend the time reciting prayers would not meet your need. You want first of all to learn more about God. How can you do it ?

Clearly, in such a situation, meditation or mental prayer is, as we have said, something very like education. Equally clearly it is something quite different. To spend the time simply on the study of theology would not be what was needed. Yet, on the other hand, knowledge, a forming of the mind, is precisely what is needed.

This gives us our first clue. There are two parts to the mind-training which enters into meditation. One part is the cooking and serving of the meal; the other is eating it. Before you begin your meditation, you must have some matter prepared.

St. Ignatius in the Exercises met this need by prescribing a preparatory quarter of an hour in which the matter was outlined in ' points ', by the priest who was guiding the person making the retreat. In the text of the book of the Exercises he supplies the actual ' points ' for the meditations of that retreat. In an ordinary modern retreat, the need is met by a sermon or conference intended to be the preparation for a period of prayer to follow. It must be admitted that many modern retreats have advanced so far that the sermon seems to be everything, and the prayer to follow is left out; as though one should go to a restaurant, order a dinner, pay for it, and go off without eating it. In the routine of many religious congregations the need is met by a prescribed period of preparation, often the night before, a preparation for meditation the following morning. Not infrequently this takes the form of a public reading of some matter presumed to be suitable for all alike. But what if one is not in retreat, or is not a religious? Even then it is vital that there should be a time of preparation, distinct from the prayer itself. In practice this will probably mean that in order to make progress in meditation, you will have to devote some regular time to reading, and from that reading, brief though it may be, gather matter for your meditation.

Then some thought, some idea, which struck you in your reading, is recalled, dwelt on, examined from new angles, linked up with previous experience, and so assimilated more firmly by the mind. Our Holy Father Pius XII recommends to us as a means for reaching some understanding of divine mysteries, the method recommended by the Vatican Council, " the method by which light is successfully sought for some partial perception of God's hidden truths in a comparison of mysteries with one another and with the last end to which they are directed ".

Thus from reading we gather some thought, some idea, which we can use in meditation. If there is one thing that is characteristic of the work of the Holy Spirit as Teacher, it is a delightful freedom from syllabuses and courses; for God is the great master of the art of opportunity, and we must not imagine that in the providential guidance which leads us to the right matter for meditation, or in the light which from time to time He throws upon special points, there will be any system that we can recognise. In other words there is no prescribed course of mental training which goes with the practice of meditation. We must seek our soul's nourishment when and where Providence disposes. And only too often it seems like shopping in a post-war period, with goods in short supply. That must not distress us. God nourishes the soul by fasts as well as feasts.

But let us repeat it: the aim of meditation is not exclusively enrichment of the mind; mental prayer is not study simply; the aim is to love God through thinking about Him. In point of fact even the sheer education of the mind can have that other prayer-value, from the intention which directs it to the glory of God; but the special value of mental prayer is attained when through the thoughts the heart—and that means essentially the will—is kindled to love of God. Hence in any period of prayer as soon as such a stirring of affection is felt, we should foster it, even to the extent of going no further along the train of thought that prompted it.

A constantly repeated point of St. Ignatius in his teaching on prayer is that as soon as the fruit is found we should gather it. This arousing of affection is one chief fruit of meditation. That is not to say that other effects of meditation are not also fruit. One of these others is more concerned with the mind than with the will: it is that seeing, grasping, penetrating of a truth, which from time to time comes to us in the course of a meditation. Some truth comes home to us. We pass from a notional to a real apprehension of it. Such an experience, such a "light" is a pleasure, a satisfaction, a consolation.

And that word consolation brings to mind one most important matter that concerns the whole of the life of prayer. We began this explanation of prayer by insisting that there is a darkness, a desolation, which is morally certain to come upon all who persevere in prayer. We mentioned that even before such a desert is reached there are likely to have been ups and downs, periods of facility alternating with periods of difficulty. Now let us say, with emphasis, that if there is one law that runs through the whole history of a life of prayer, it is this law of up-and-down. More characteristically of prayer than of any other development, it is the rule that progress is like the progress of an incoming tide, that each forward movement is followed by a backward one, and that if on the whole the tide rises along the shore, the pre-dominant impression is one of constant withdrawal after each advance, and the total advance is imperceptible or unperceived. These alternations of up and down are usually called consolation and desolation.

St. Ignatius in one place[5] defines consolation as any increase of faith, hope and charity. It is also important to notice that the connotation or meaning of the word —what it stands for in terms of real experience—changes according to the changing phases of the development of prayer. It is like the meaning of the word recreation ; at all times of life recreation means recreation, but what we consider recreation at fifteen we would not consider recreation at fifty ; at fifty a gentle walk along a grassy slope, perhaps with the added interest of a bag of clubs and a little white ball, will fill the bill admirably as recreation, and we should view with consternation the proposal that we should do the things we did with so much zest in the freshness of fifteen. So too with prayer : the thrill of a new discovery in the realm of ideas is consolation to a beginner ; later on there will be no such discoveries, nor would they bring the same thrill if there were. In early years consolation is almost synonymous with emotional sweetness; later our taste so changes that we should not care very much for such emotion even if it were within our reach.

Meditation, then, especially in its earlier phases, is a matter eminently concerned with education or formation of the mind. It consists, in essential part, of proposing to the mind ideas and truths for assimilation. According to personal bent or taste the manner of the proposing will vary. Some minds are attracted by abstractions and find their delight in dwelling on virtues, arranging, classifying, analysing them; for such an admirable source of matter for meditation would be the *Summa Theologica* of St. Thomas Aquinas, especially the *Secunda Secundae*. In that orderly exposition they will find much guidance and inspiration for the moulding of their own lives and characters.

Others, doubtless the majority, most readily grasp reality when it is presented in the form of human story. For them the sovereign fountain of guidance and inspiration is the life of Christ, either in the majestic simplicity of the Gospel itself, or in the many studies of the life that have been based upon the Gospel. For them other plentiful sources are to be found in the biographies of men and women who have followed Christ, whether in the fascinating strangeness of a remote past or in the familiar setting of contemporary life.

For these especially the technique of presenting to the mind matter for meditation is much assisted by making use of the imagination. We are endowed by nature with five senses, by means of which we are made aware of the material world around us; but we are also equipped with a marvellous recording system, by which the manifold abundance of experience is stored, and can be brought before our consciousness almost at will. Moreover it can be remoulded and recombined with a freedom that is creative. This is done by the imagination.

When we wish to meditate on some story or event,

perhaps from the life of Our Lord, we can put before the mind a moving picture, complete with sound-track, of the scene. The purpose of this is not only to shut out other distracting memories, which the imagination if not occupied tends to put forward ; it is also to ensure that our reaching up to God engages our entire self, sense and intelligence, emotion and will. And for many it is precisely through such a vivid, three-dimensional grasp of historic actuality that the intellect best perceives truth. Most of us, in other words, like to learn by looking out of the window ; and in these days especially when so much of our impression of the world comes through films and picture-papers, it is very necessary to canalise that energy and harness it to the task of reaching God through prayer. Our Lord became Man for this among other purposes, that we might be able to see and hear the living God with the eyes and ears of our body. And since we are not living during His lifetime, we can at least secure a measure of that vividness of apprehension which actually seeing and hearing Him would have given, by using the recording apparatus of memory and imagination.

For this purpose accuracy of detail is valuable, but it must be understood as the artists understand it ; it does not matter very much whether our imaginative picture of the cave at Bethlehem corresponds exactly in size and shape to the real one ; what does matter is that it should be a clear and definite picture, capable of holding our attention and leading us on to penetration of spiritual truth. It is of course desirable that we should know the historical facts if they are available ; but the position is like that concerning films : it is better that if possible a historical film should be historically accurate, but even more important for the success of the film is that it should be good photography ; blurred images badly lighted will be less effectual, even if they satisfy the antiquaries in their details, than a good picture, true in substance but drawing upon the imagination for its minutiae. For the purposes of imagination as an aid to mental prayer, it is a historical novel, rather than a thesis for a doctorate, which is helpful.

Some people are devoid of the power of visual imagination. For them the attempt to assist mental prayer by the use of pictures in the mind is a waste of time. They are blessedly free from one very pertinacious source of distractions. Usually they will notice that the defect in visual imagination is compensated for by greater ability in the other imaginative senses ; they may be unable to see a scene, but very much able to hear in imagination the dialogue of the scene ; their aid to mental prayer may be rather a radio play than a film. More probably their bent will be towards an abstract or intellectual approach, and they will find their handicap a help, not only in sparing them distracting images but also in making easier for them a more purely spiritual grasp of truth.

So to sum up : if you wish to make mental prayer an integral and constant element in your life, if you wish to grow in the knowledge and love of Our Lord and in union with the Divine Majesty and Goodness, you will be well advised to begin with the methodical practice of meditation. Your first need will probably be for a deeper education of the mind, and while no one suggests that such education, apart from the love of God, is in the true sense prayer, common sense shows that you cannot pull with a rope until you have a rope ; prayer which begins by being spiritual education is necessary.

VI

AFFECTIVE PRAYER

But how long is this to last ? How long does prayer continue to be a process notably educative and formative for the mind ? Manifestly we shall not in all the length of eternity exhaust the inexhaustible treasures of the infinite wonder of God. Prayer is not merely a training, but a life—*the* life. It is the drinking of those living waters which wholly satisfy yet never cloy, which even in quenching the thirst arouse an ever intenser thirst. But prayer, being a created life, is a growth, and as a growth passes through phases and changes. In particular there is an end, relatively speaking, of the merely intellectual formation and education. There comes a time when meditation in the restricted sense of reasonings and human discoveries comes to a standstill. That desert land which was the subject of our opening pages was an image of such a standstill. In speaking of it we said that in bringing it to pass the Holy Spirit made use in part of the operation of secondary causes. That is to say, the process of meditation by its own natural laws will tend to come to an end, even if no supernatural influence enters in to bring it to an end. Let us now consider why this is so.

But first consider what is the natural and normal evolution of any process of acquiring knowledge. Take for instance getting to know a person or becoming familiar with a town. At first there is a time of observation and discovery; facts are noted and correlated; we walk through the town, noting landmarks, finding how one street leads unexpectedly into another that we knew already, how a curve where we imagined the road was straight alters our whole conception of the lay-out; or with a person we observe mannerisms, expressions, tones of voice, reactions, lines of thought. During this time of observation and discovery the sheer emergence of new facts gives us pleasure; it is a delight just to get to know. But that time passes. Without our being aware of it, the sum of our experience of the person or the place shakes itself down and settles into a unity or a totality; thereafter the mention of the name recalls to us a generalised, somewhat confused, but unified and total awareness of the person or place. It is not a human habit, when thinking of our friends, to continue indefinitely an analytical study of them such as we apply to new acquaintances.

Or again, the process of study of a science goes through similar phases. There comes a time, not when we sit back and fold our arms saying 'Now I know all that there is to be known about that', but when we are satisfied that we have a comprehensive grasp of the whole; when what remains is the fuller grasp of detail, which will enter into an outline adequately complete, but when the first delight of discovery and exploration is over.

Notice, it is not precisely that we feel we have exhausted the science we were coming to know; it is rather that we feel we have satisfied our own capacity for knowledge. Our appetite is sated.

So it is with meditation. There comes a point when our natural capacity for absorbing the truths of God's revelation, as presented to us in intelligible language through the teaching of Christ and His Church, has reached a saturation-point. The sponge is full. It is not that there is no more water in the ocean, but the sponge has absorbed what it needs. Our natural intellectual grasp of religion has reached a stage when it is ready to shake itself down and settle into a unity or totality, when discovery and exploration are no longer such a pleasure, and what we seek for is something like the post-prandial beatitude which prefers digestion to the study of further menus.

In the ordinary course of things, therefore, it is to be expected that meditation in the sense of methodical, analytic study of sacred truths, will not continue for a lifetime. Doubtless there are exceptions; but a person who can continue this kind of meditative ratiocination all through a lifetime is surely something of a rarity. Normal folks are likely to find that however methodically they begin, and however successful they may be at first

in proceeding logically from point to point, their awareness of the sum of Christian revelation in prayer passes
imperceptibly into a more comprehensive but less sharply
defined grasp of the whole : like a broad sea, on the
surface of which waves mount and fall unpredictably,
waves of momentary thought touching now on this truth
now on that, but touching swiftly, as it were in passing,
not so much analysing an idea as intuitively perceiving
it and all its ramifications and connections with other
ideas, all the time deepening and strengthening the
apprehension of the whole.

It is this unification, this simplification, this ' simple
regard ', which may normally be expected to be the next
stage in the evolution of the mental factor in prayer.
And it is probable that such a generalised awareness of
Christian truth and of the personality of Our Lord will
be accompanied by a similarly diffused, contented, happy
emotional state, in which momentary waves of affectionate impulse sparkle on the sea of the soul, like waves
on a sunlit ocean lively in the play of a dancing wind
—following in fact the unpredictable and inconsequent
shimmer of thoughts that enlighten the mind and are gone
like sun-glints before they can be seized. Prayer becomes
" affective ". The rope is taut, and humming with quiet
contentment, as a taut rope may. This affective joy is
in the feelings, the emotions, the sensitive part of the
personality ; it is a symptom or an index of a deeper
spiritual joy in the will, a joy not yet clearly perceived,
because masked by the scintillations of the surface, for
one cannot see down into the water when the surface
is moving and glittering. In order that the deep,
unshakable joy may become a conscious possession of
the personality, it will be necessary for all that superficial
delight to pass away ; the history of a life of prayer is
the emergence into consciousness of secret forces rising
from the innermost recesses of the soul.

Such a warmth and sunlit contentment in prayer will
readily be recognised as " consolation ". Prayer is easy

when such is its quality. The difficulty is to believe, when this has passed away, that something else is in future to be what we shall recognise as " consolation " ; to see that when one becomes a man one must, with St. Paul, put away the things of child, and that to cling to this consolation, excellent thing though it is, is a subtle form of self-attachment, the fault of a spiritual *gourmet* if not that of a spiritual *gourmand*.

Undoubtedly, when prayer is thus lapped in comforts, it is easy to be good ; at any rate it appears so. But, as Père de Grandmaison remarked, this affective prayer, even when the focus of it is the felt presence of God, " pallie nos defauts plus qu'il ne les mortifie " ; it veils our faults more than it uproots them.[6] For a time we are being " spoilt ", and Our Lord chooses not to remind us of our weaknesses rather than to urge us to overcome them. Gradually we may even begin to notice that such affective prayer, especially if more intensely emotional, does tire us ; and we notice that the more enthusiastically we key ourselves up to emotional resolutions in prayer, convinced that now at last, after such intense determination, we are never again going to slip into our pet frailties, the more splashily do we lapse into them immediately afterwards. Such a disappointment, playing on a hidden self-attachment, a pride which has sucked strength from the conceited fancy that now we are really becoming souls of prayer, may easily lead to disaster. We begin to slack off prayer because it is exhausting and apparently useless ; and we go on to slack off the effort to be good, because that is very exhausting and bitterly flavoured with disillusion if it is not fruitless. The safeguard against this danger is detachment from oneself : the paramount aim of prayer is not the enjoyment of consolations ; it is not even our own growth in holiness ; it is the worship of God.

VII

SIGNS OF CHANGE

BUT while the way of prayer is passing through the meadows of this simplicity it is a pleasant path to tread. How long does this last? To that question the most important answer is that there are no golden rules; the one thing that can be confidently said about prayer is that there are as many histories as there are souls; lives of prayer differ from each other as much as lives in the ordinary sense, and in describing successive phases we are doing no more than we do when we distinguish ordinary lives into infancy, adolescence, maturity, middle age, old age and senility; there is no thought of determining the length of any phase in a particular instance. A map of prayer is a diagram, less applicable to a particular instance than a diagram of London's Underground is applicable to the actual lay-out of London itself.

Only in the most general terms can we say that the way will lie along these meadows just as long as the individual soul has need of that sheltering. Likewise the earlier phase of more analytic ratiocination will depend, for its duration, very much on the calibre and previous formation of the mind. It is improbable nowadays that anyone will begin a consistent practice of meditation before being fairly well instructed in Christian doctrine. If a young girl, for instance, entering a convent, finds in a relatively short time that step-by-step meditation, in which the mind deliberately examines the truths of revelation in discursive fashion, seems to be not only unattractive but even impossible, that may well be because the saturation-point, the point at which her intelligence has absorbed as much as it required of this nourishment, had been reached by her earlier, as the result of a thorough and protracted education in Christian doctrine. Alternatively the phenomenon may be due to laziness. It is difficult to be sure. Great humility and sincerity must be brought to the deciding of the question; but not an obstinate conviction that everyone who finds discursive reasoning difficult, and even imaginative rumination fruitless, is necessarily sunk in sloth. The saturation point is a very personal affair; broadly speaking it is the complex result of three factors, the calibre or brain-power of the mind, the preceding efficiency of mental formation, and the degree of supernatural development which the Holy Ghost designs. All these are virtually incalculable, notably the last, and as other secondary factors enter in, such as health, other occupations outside prayer, and special gifts like a poetic turn of mind, it is impossible to be mathematical in one's calculations. The only safe line to follow is to try and be docile to the delicate impulses of the Holy Spirit, working away at eliminating attachment to self in its increasingly subtle manifestations and endeavouring neither to rush ahead of grace nor to lag behind it.

But however long or short the period during which actively analytic or discursive meditation remains a possibility and a pleasure, or the more concretely imaginative story-telling, picture-making, continues to be a profitable ' fourth strand ' in prayer, it is morally certain that this will end. The change, as we noted earlier, is likely to be unobserved. It is likely to be masked by a period of falling-off from the enthusiastic practice of meditation, and it is often enough on the occasion of a renewal of fervour, leading to a desire to recapture the first fine careless rapture, that the difficulty of making a meditation, or what St. Ignatius would call a contemplation (imaginative musing on a scene) is first actually felt.

This difficulty may of course be due merely to some unnoticed condition of fatigue, perhaps merely to the cooling off of interest occasioned by the continued use of the kind of 'fourth strand'. The remedy in such a case might well be to turn to the " Second method of prayer " proposed by St. Ignatius, and shepherd our straying thoughts by choosing a sequence of words, such as some verses of the Gospel, and repeating them slowly, with a pause after each word, for the content of that word to sink slowly into the mind, like honey into bread. This is a method of prayer about which we shall have more to say.

But although sometimes the lack of facility in meditation or 'Ignatian contemplation' is merely a seasonal phenomenon, like the disappearance of parish choirs during the summer months, and the remedy lies in a more energetic return to meditation, it is not always so. We would go further and say that for every normal person there comes a time when it is not so. Some subsidiary signs may be given which lend confidence in presuming that we have reached that time. One is this : it is the sharp contrast, earlier alluded to, between the facility we experience in seeing vistas of thought or sketching lines of meditation while we are preparing the matter for meditation, and the sudden fall—as of a curtain—of a cloudy inability to think at all, which descends upon us when the time for meditation comes. Similar to this is a longing, almost a gnawing eagerness, which we feel for prayer, so long as it is impossible for us to give our undivided attention to it, this being sharply contrasted with a feeling of boredom and distaste that comes upon us as soon as we are free to give ourselves to prayer. The longing sometimes takes the form of an abundance of affectionate impulses, or 'sensible consolation', which persist in the midst of other activities and vanish the moment we come to prayer, as if they were one of those optical illusions that we can only see by not looking at them. Another form which the first of these signs takes is that while prayer itself remains as it were paralysed, while it is devoid of any light that we can recognise as being a deeper understanding of the familiar truths of faith, such a light does seem to be growing in the soul outside the time of prayer, and more especially during spiritual reading.

Not only, then, do these signs, if they are present, afford us some assurance that the blankness of our prayer is not the effects of our sloth, but they also provide us with another clue for the explanation of what is happening in prayer. The outline history of the evolution of prayer is the emergence into the realm of consciousness of powers of knowledge latent at first below the surface; but it is also the process by which those emerging powers influence the natural ways of knowledge employed from the outset. To understand the full development let us examine an image, or concept, which we can use as an illustration to throw light on the process. It is the image or concept of " carriers ". The fourth strand of prayer we likened to a length of flex; the insulating cover " carried " the metal core, and the metal core " carried " the current. Let us examine the relation between those natural thoughts or ideas in which our mental prayer, so far as it is 'a kind of knowing or consciousness, appeared at first to consist, and the emerging super-natural element which was " carried " by those ideas.

VIII

CARRIERS

THERE is a moment in the life of the ordinary mortal which is of great significance, though it is not always observed even by the fond mammas and papas who inflict upon the neighbours circumstantial accounts of the doings of their progeny. It is the moment when the small child, playing with its bricks, pushes forward two bricks, considers them intently, and looking up says " Two ". It is the moment when a truly abstract idea has been disengaged from the concrete and waved about triumphantly by the majestic reasoning power of man —aged three perhaps. But the little man will wave it about by means of the word " Two ", or some other concrete symbol, which serves for a communication with other men. That does not alter the fact that he has grasped an abstract idea, but it does illustrate the other fact that for us mortals ideas are almost necessarily clothed in some embodying expression. We think ' *per conversionem ad phantasma* '. The poet's eye in a fine frenzy rolling gives to airy nothings a local habitation and a name. And that embodying expression, that phantasm that makes the concept apprehensible, that local habitation that houses the airy nothing, is a " carrier " for the idea.

Likewise the idea itself is a carrier for the still more rarefied and spiritual perception of divine truth of which the supernatural life makes us capable.

Again, language, the spoken or written word, is the carrier of meaning. The aim of education, wisely understood, is to train men to grasp through language the treasures of meaning. For this it is first of all necessary that attention should be devoted to the language itself, a fact which is patent when we consider how little children are taught to read. But if the education is a wise one, the aim will thereafter be almost the reverse ; it will be to lead the mind to separate the word from the thing, and it will be to coax it forward to a more and more intellectual grasp of truth and to the recognition that material things are the least real of things, not, as our senses incline us to believe, the only real things. Education will lead on from the concrete to the abstract, and from the material to the spiritual. Now the work of the Holy Spirit, the Master of Prayer, is to coax us further still, up to the apprehension of what is beyond the powers of reason, up to the supernatural. Therefore just as it is necessary, in all the ascensions of the ladder of knowledge, deliberately to take away attention from a lower rung in order to rise to the higher which we have reached by means of the lower—as when we forget the style of print to attend to the meaning, or as when we endeavour to ignore the phantasm in order to grasp the metaphysical concept—so is it necessary for the Holy Spirit to blindfold us to our natural mental grasp of truth in order to direct our attention to the emerging supernatural apprehension. That is what He is doing when the strange paralysis settles upon our minds in prayer.

But just as a fine perception of meaning need not finally prevent us from appreciating beauty of language, or even beauty of printing and bookbinding, so the darkness that covers the mind in prayer is a temporary stage, and finally we shall be given back our full natural apprehension of that book of God's creation wherein He, the Meaning, is written.

Moreover as a finer perception of meaning itself increases appreciation of beauty of language—after the momentary inattention to it which the reaching forward to deeper meaning has necessitated—so the growth in us of the supernatural light increases our natural knowledge. This is that reflected light falling upon the natural powers of the mind, that effect of faith enabling us to grasp more securely the Christian revelation in its human expression, and to see more clearly God imaged in the world ; this we suggested was the effect of the Gift of the Holy Ghost called Understanding.[7]

Thus it sometimes happens that in the very period in which we feel most crushingly our inability to meditate in prayer, we experience most strikingly a light upon our thoughts outside prayer.

And this emphasises the importance of a point made earlier : there are two factors involved in the practice of mental prayer, in so far as it is an activity of the power of knowing (it should be remembered that the full prayer consists of knowing and loving) ; one is the preparation of matter for meditation, the other is the using of the matter prepared. Now even when it ceases to be possible to use, by any sort of discursive activity, during the actual time of prayer, the matter prepared beforehand, we should nevertheless go on preparing it. For this 'preparation' increasingly takes on the character and function of the nourishing and educating of the mind, in proportion as the time of prayer itself is more exclusively devoted to the developing of the supernatural powers. As presented by St. Ignatius in his methodical instructions, the two processes are closely fused or identified; but with the evolution of prayer they are liable to become separated. It is important to remember that both are to continue. A life of prayer without 'spiritual reading' will be in danger. And in normal circumstances it is from 'spiritual reading' rather than directly from prayer that we gather the scanty sheaves which we have to make into bread if it is our duty to instruct others, and provide "in tempore tritici mensuram".[8] For what we can communicate to others must necessarily be what can be grasped by the natural powers. The far more precious supernatural illumination only God Himself can give.[9]

Moreover the constant and faithful practice of preparing matter intended to occupy the natural powers of thought during prayer is valuable for another reason, connected immediately with the prayer itself. The reason is this: while it is a relatively good thing that the focus of attention should be directed to a supernatural level of awareness, and that for that purpose a certain temporary blindness or stupor should cloud attention to thought at the level of everyday reasoning, it is only relatively good, *bonum secundum quid* as the Scholastics say, good from one point of view. It is good in the way in which illness or pain is good—in itself not-good, but capable of being used by Almighty God for a good purpose. And just as it would be wrong for us to make ourselves ill, or to neglect ordinary means of health, even though sickness is a gift of God and in His hands an instrument of good, so would it be an error for us in prayer to seek imprudently the emptiness and blur of thought which may in the hands of God be a potent aid to the development of the supernatural powers. Our normal business is to do what we can to prevent that emptiness from coming to us, as it is our normal business to take moderate care of our health; there are of course exceptions; St. John of the Cross who seems to urge us to take active steps to induce the complete suspension of ordinary mental activity in prayer,[10] is prescribing for persons in whom it is evident that the Holy Spirit is preparing a very full flowering of supernatural prayer.[11] For the rank and file of the army of prayer, the cautious attitude of doing all that we can to facilitate the natural activities in prayer is wise, because, as previously hinted, it is not easy to distinguish between laziness and an inertia over which we have no control; it is safer to assume, until the contrary is clear, that we ourselves are as lazy as the next man.

Thought that focuses the normal levels of attention upon God's revelation, upon some truth that has been shown us through Christ Our Lord, is the ordinary ' carrier ' of that supernatural awareness which is the further aim of Christian prayer. Such thought provides in ordinary circumstances the ' contact ', the transmitting agent, which communicates to us this awareness, imperceptible in itself to the natural powers. In early stages the thought is deliberately elaborated, so as to hold the attention of the ordinary thinking-apparatus; gradually, as we have described, it tends of itself to become simpler or more intuitive; and progressively it concentrates itself upon nodal points, for instance upon a word or a phrase—' Jesus ! ', ' My God and my all ! '—or upon an image or symbolic idea, such as the idea, felt rather than pictured, of the enfolding of the soul in the arms of the Eternal Father, or upon a fixed and stable sequence of vignettes of meditation—" My God I believe in You . . . I am glad You are what You are . . . I rejoice in your glory . . . in the Father's love of the Son . . . in the Son's return to the Father "—such nodal points proving in experience to be, while that period of consolation lasts, the most effective ' contacts ' for our entry into the presence of God.

When these carriers or contacts are given to us, in the sense that we hardly seek them but they seem to present themselves to us, the time of preparation for prayer is devoted more to spiritual reading as a form of further instruction of the powers of the mind at their normal levels of operation. But it will be often found that it is here and there, unpredictably, in that spiritual reading that we come upon jewels which in their turn prove to be nodal points or contacts for our prayer, and that to abandon the spiritual reading on the plea that we needed no further matter for our meditation might lead to a dryness in which we lost the awareness of God in prayer.

This, then, is the image or analogy which we have been elaborating, the image of carriers ; that as signs, words, language, poetic metaphor and other means of communication are vehicles which carry meaning, as air is the vehicle of sound and the ether (if it exists) the medium for light, as the metal wires transmit electric current and biological cells endowed with life are centres for the spreading of life to other organisations of matter, so human thought is the vehicle for the development of a supernatural mode of knowledge in the soul of man. It is the carrier, not the thing itself. The evolution of prayer is the unfolding of the new life, and we are considering it almost exclusively at the moment from its aspect as a form of knowledge, though we are fully aware of the fact that it is not the knowledge but the love that matters—not the rope but the pull on the rope. The evolution is an unfolding, as of a flower.

That unfolding, as achieved through mental prayer, leads first to an enriching, an education, of the mind. Gradually this enriching takes on a more supernatural character as the light of Faith illumines our ideas of the world and of God's action in the world. But it is relatively secondary : the chief objective of the development is not to make us better able to understand God's work, but to lead us towards God Himself. Hence it is that the growth of mental prayer converges upon one central fact, the fact that God exists, that God is God, that God is present in our souls, and that the one thing necessary for us as conscious beings is the increasing apprehension of this sovereign truth. Hence it is that prayer tends to simplify itself towards awareness of the presence of God, and that the growing-point of a truly fruitful life of prayer is the emergence into consciousness of a ' sense ' of that presence, a ' taste ', a ' touch '—we have to use words borrowed from the vocabulary of everyday life because there are no new words for the new thing, and by instinct Christian tradition has inclined towards names taken from the five senses, to suggest the immediacy, the intuitive directness, of this experience of the presence of God.[12] The keynote of supernatural prayer has always been recognised as this : an experienced awareness of the presence or the reality of God.[13] The word ' experimental ' is often used for ' experienced '; this is misleading for us to whom a thing is said to be experimental when we are trying it and have not permanently adopted it ; ' experiential ' is perhaps a less confusing word.

There is, in the nature of the case, no adequate parallel to suggest, to one who does not know by personal experience, what is this 'sense' of the presence of God. One might compare it with the state of mind experienced in a railway compartment when the train is going through a tunnel with no lights on, and there is another person in the compartment ; though we neither see nor hear nor touch the person, our knowledge of the fact that someone is there may give us an impression of the impact of a personality on our consciousness. But this utterly inadequate comparison can give no idea of the thing.

Inevitably not, because God is quite different from all other beings, and because the awareness of Himself He grants in prayer is something different from our natural mode of knowing.

In such a phase of prayer, what we receive by supernatural gift is simply the realisation that God exists, or that He is close to us. We know *that* He is, not *what* He is. But this realisation is carried in a matrix of thoughts and ideas about God, truths learnt through revelation and the teaching of the Church, and the realisation itself, as we have previously described, throws a new light upon those thoughts and ideas. Hence there is an inclination to fancy that we are really coming to know *what* God is, to imagine that we are advancing in the mystic way and receiving revelations from on high. This inclination is not unconnected with our own conceit and attachment to self. It is not in the least necessary that we should be able to tell whether our ideas about God have come from our previous education or from a special illumination from above; our business is to love God in all humility, and gladly to accept whatever form of light He grants us concerning Himself, without childish curiosity about which rung of the ladder we are on. But if we are troubled by such curiosity it is well to remember that the beginning of mystical prayer, properly so called, is a cloud of unknowing; and that if we can express to ourselves the knowledge of God we have acquired in our prayer, that in itself is sufficient to show that the ideas have come through the ordinary powers of the mind and are something quite different from what the mystics are talking about.

Sometimes, in like manner, it may seem to us in moments of consolation that Our Lord has spoken in our souls; that some message of assurance has come to us with a quality that makes it difficult to doubt that the assurance was from Him. The best thing to do is to notice whether the ' message ' is not already expressed in His revelation. It usually is. It may be for instance

56

an intense conviction of the reality of His special love for us. Then we can say to Him: "I do not know whether it was my imagination that seemed to whisper this to me; I do not know if it was You who made use of my imagination; what I do know is that You have told me this through your Church; You have assured me in Scripture that You have loved me and delivered Yourself for me, that You have loved me with an everlasting love; thank You for the vividness with which that moment in prayer brought home this truth to me; I believe it because You have said it through Your Church."

If the 'message' happens to be a special instruction to be another Joan of Arc or found a new religious congregation, Scripture gives no guidance on such particular points, and you will do well to assume that it comes from an over-heated imagination, until by some exterior guidance God makes His will clear.

But ordinarily prayer in the phase we are now speaking about is principally concerned with the paramount, sovereign fact that God exists, and the immediate practical problem is how to keep ourselves in His presence, how to sustain that awareness of His presence which is for us the treasure of treasures.

IX

DISTRACTIONS AND "DOING NOTHING"

WE have outlined the normal tendency towards a state in which that sense of the presence is attained by the use of simple 'contacts'. It must have been something similar to this which could keep a St. Francis praying through the night and saying only 'My Lord and my God'. The famous old man who when asked what he did all the time in prayer replied 'I look at Him and He looks at me', must have been finding in the simple renewal of that glance of the imagination the means of renewing his sense of the presence of God. For most of us, perhaps, the process resembles nothing so much as the pertinacity of Robert Bruce's spider, or those engaging little celluloid balls that rise and continually fall down again on jets of water in shooting galleries : no sooner has the poor thing begun to mount steadily on the jet than it is off again. So does prayer for many, and perhaps for a long, long time, become a patient process of continually starting again. No sooner have we succeeded in focusing our thoughts on something that we hope will prove a ' contact ' than away they go chasing some will-o'-the-wisp, and we wake up some time later from a day-dream of distractions.

And this seems to get worse. When it does, it is a help to realise that it is just what we ought to expect ; it fits in quite explicably with the situation as a whole. Distractions will become more uncontrollable, and may take on the characteristics of dreams, being inconsequent, absurd, and somehow not belonging to us even though they are going on in our own heads. The reason is that these distractions are like dreams in the sense that they are involuntary as far as our will is concerned, and they go by their own momentum, like a railway-truck on a shunting slope, and that our focus of attention is too much occupied with trying to reach the sense of the presence of God to have very much vigour left for controlling the automatic distractions. If the awareness of God were vivid, that would overcome the wandering of the mind ; if the occupation of the mind were meditation in the discursive sense, that would conflict directly with the distractions and either overcome them, or be overcome by them ; but the situation in which the attention is chiefly taken up with groping for the realisation of God's presence, without finding it, leaves the way open for a free-wheeling of the mind that is very distressing. To add to our distress, the failure to enjoy the sense of God's presence, often coupled with a failure to fix the mind even for two moments on any thought that might provide the contact, makes us feel that we are doing nothing, and that our so-called prayer is nothing but a waste of time and an insult to Almighty God.

It is as if the earlier kind of meditation consisted in sitting in a house looking out at the garden through the drawing-room windows, admiring the sunlight on the lawn, with the children behaving reasonably, busying themselves over hobbies and toys. Then comes an invitation from the Holy Spirit to go up to the attic and look out through the skylight. Our first reaction may be a realisation of the brightness of the sunlight. Our second, after a while, is likely to be the remark ' I can't see anything '. Then from downstairs comes the noise of the children romping in our absence. Looking at the garden in the sunlight was meditation, of the kind that interests and occupies the mind, providing it with what suits its own capacities. We grow so accustomed to seeing objects in light that we forget it is primarily the light itself that we see ; it is the light that affects our retinas. So we are accustomed to meditate on things, which our mind perceives because in one way or another light from the source of all light, the un-created Being of God, falls upon them and is reflected into our minds. We grow so much accustomed to this that we rarely realise it at all. But God wants us to realise the presence of the light, that is of Himself ; more particularly He wants us to realise the presence of the special supernatural rays which He is conditioning our souls to respond to. Therefore He invites us to the attic, through the skylight of which we " see nothing ", because through that skylight we are not looking at any things on which the light of God is falling, but are looking towards God Himself. We see nothing—except light. This is what God wants ; He wishes us to turn our attention fully to the awareness of His presence which is beginning to penetrate into our consciousness.

Meanwhile the children romp; that is, the automatism of trains of thought, especially such as have emotional force, asserts itself, and it becomes more difficult than ever to control distractions.

It is very necessary not to be stampeded and panicked by the cry that rises in our hearts " I am doing nothing ". One simple proof that we are not doing nothing is to stop doing it: provided that in spite of appearances we really have been endeavouring to reach the awareness of God, then the cessation of this endeavour will be observed as the cessation of a monotonous sound is observed even though we have grown so used to the sound that we have ceased to notice it. For the endeavour to reach God in this way, when properly understood and practised, contains within itself a movement or attitude of the will, which is love, and loving God in this way is not " doing nothing ", however like it it may seem. And, it might be added, a sentry on duty is not doing nothing even if there is ' not a mouse stirring ', provided that he remains alert and on the watch. " Watch and pray ", said Our Lord. There comes a time when the two terms blend into one and prayer becomes almost exclusively watching and waiting.

But all this presupposes that we are doing something even if that something is the imperceptible stillness of a sentry on duty. If at a certain point distractions can acquire a dreamlike distantness which does not seriously interfere with the steady reaching out of the soul towards God, at an earlier point they can certainly interfere with it and check the current altogether. The phase we are describing is one in which there is an uneasy balance of conflicting appeals to the attention. If through real laziness we yield to the free-wheeling of the mind and allow our prayer to become an unresisting float down the river of day-dreams, then the supernatural awareness of God will never grow. It remains, here as elsewhere, difficult to distinguish off-hand the good from the bad, laziness from active stillness. We need sincerity and humility, combined with a common-sense prudence that will not be stampeded into a panic. Distractions, more especially during such a phase of prayer as this, have to be resisted firmly and patiently, but gently.

X

THE BODY IN PRAYER

AND this suggests another matter that ought to be mentioned: it is the part that the body plays in our prayer. We are prone to think of ourselves, where anything like religion is concerned, as being just what we are so often called in spiritual books—souls ; we forget that we are a union of soul and body forming a person.

Ramon Lull in *The Art of Contemplation*[14] counsels the avoidance of " repletion and overmuch grieving " and of " places wherein is bustle or noise, or excess of heat and cold ". In other words, mental prayer as such does depend to some extent on bodily conditions. Notice, it is not prayer, in the broad sense of that co-operation with God which unites us to Him, that depends on these accidental circumstances. A martyr on the rack would not be able to achieve mental prayer, except by an almost miraculous assistance from God ; but he would be offering the sublimest of all prayers, the prayer of Christ on the Cross. Ordinary folk in ordinary conditions, debarred by bustle and noise or excess of heat and cold from achieving any mental prayer, are not on that account cut off from God. But for those for whom Divine Providence has made possible some achievement of prayer in the manner of which we are speaking, the body is a factor not to be ignored.

St. Ignatius advises[15] that before beginning any period of prayer we should pause, standing for the space of an *Our Father*, a pace or two from the spot where we are going to pray, and recalling the presence of Our Lord Who is watching what we are about to do ; then we should make an act of reverence and self-abasement. The primary purpose of this recommendation is evidently the psychological state of mind, recollectedness, awareness of Christ's attention to us, reverence. But it is also evident that the advice concerns bodily attitude ; the *Versio Vulgata* of the *Exercises* gives the paraphrase ' reverentiam cum humili gestu exhibere '—*gestus* applies to an outward, corporeal movement. " Les attitudes cr ent les tats de l'esprit " ;[16] and if this is more manifest in such action-prayer as the liturgy, it is also of importance even in prayer that is predominantly concerned with the interior consciousness. To pray well, even in the sense of meditating well, we should put ourselves into a posture of body that will assist the mind. The obvious and natural position for us in Western Europe is kneeling. It is best if possible to kneel down ; but if we do we should also kneel up : curvature of the spine, even when gracefully attained over an upholstered prie-dieu, does not make for lasting stillness ; it is better to have the dorsal vertebrae one above the other. But kneeling is not indispensable ; there must be reverence of mind, and it is well if it is expressed by reverence of body, but for purposes of mental prayer it is desirable that we should be able to forget the body, and if poor ' Brother Ass ' is twitching with discomfort he will decline to be forgotten. It may be necessary for us to sit. It may also be necessary simply to change position or to move about, as a relief from weariness, as a safety-valve for nervous tension, or as a cure for drowsiness. But the one thing that is pre-eminently required for the development of mental or interior prayer is quiet. And I would suggest as a routine entry into prayer a practice founded on the recommendation of St. Ignatius mentioned above, and envisaging more especially the needs of our nerve-shattered age. I will call it the practice of the Three Quiets : quiet of body, quiet of heart, and quiet of mind.

XI

THREE QUIETS

THERE can be little question that in Western civilisation to-day we are living in a state of unremitting nervous tension that is quite unnatural and probably unprecedented. It is not that we are living in fear of major cataclysms like wars ; people in other ages may have had greater reason to fear serious danger to themselves. It is the unrelenting pressure of hurry—skimming the newspaper headlines, running for the train, trying to keep abreast of the stream of events and the torrent of literature, all these and a thousand and one other prickles make up the hair-shirt of present-day existence. Hence our desperate need in approaching prayer is first of all a relaxing of nervous tension.

Begin then, I suggest, with quiet of body. Kneel, or sit, and be still. Let go the nerves. Relax the muscles. Stop mistaking a series of melancholy sighs for a sensible manner of breathing, and breathe like a human being, that is, forget all about it. Throw off the interior whalebone that emotional anxiety or petty resentment has introduced somewhere in the region of the chest. Smile : or at least allow the facial muscles to resume whatever attractiveness nature meant them to give way to in repose. Unclench the teeth. Try in general to attain a state of calm and restfulness in the nervous system before beginning to pray at all.

After quiet of body, quiet of heart. 'After' means that we mention it next, not necessarily that it comes next in time ; it may have to come first. The disturbances that most deeply trouble our peace are those which

cause emotional reactions ; and these are almost univers-
ally things that touch the raw nerve of our self-attachment,
that self-love of the wrong kind which we all have
in us. Tiffs, petty injustices, slights, small successes
that tickle vanity, conversations—in our own heads—
with people with whom we are annoyed, and whom we
devastate—in our own heads—with crushing and un-
answerable rejoinders, worries and the ways and means
with which we must meet them : all these and many
similar things are like brambles that catch and tear at
our emotions. Quiet of heart means putting them out
of mind. The way to do it is detachment. Detachment
means realising that God alone matters, that everything
is in His hands and if we care for Him out of all comparison with anything else, all will be well ; we can leave
those things to Him ; this ' quiet of heart ' should be
a mere glance in the direction of the particular bugbear
that is chasing us at the moment, followed by a swift
advance backwards in the other direction. The snag
to be circumvented is that the mere recalling of the
current bête-noir is liable to launch us into an all-in
struggle with it ; but it is worth risking this in order
to put the bête-noir firmly out of mind, because there is
even more likelihood of its worming its way into our
thoughts uninvited if we do not. Quiet of heart means
a deliberate disentangling of ourselves from emotional
brambles.

Then quiet of mind. What this will mean will depend
very much on the character of our prayer in general
at the moment. It may mean anything from a full
systematic presentation to the mind of a complete
Ignatian methodical approach, introductory prayer,
composition of place and points in brief review, to a
simple reaching for the ' contact ' which at that time
is helping us to enter into the sense of the presence of
God, or an even simpler plunging immediately into
wordless adoration. But it means in general disengaging
the attention from other lines of thought and devoting it

as completely as possible to God or to thoughts that will lead us to God.

I would suggest this routine approach especially to those who find that the common stumbling-block at the beginning of prayer is the impossibility of staying still. Even, however, if the practice works, and we succeed in coaxing ourselves into stillness and quiet, it is very probable that the said quiet will last about as long as the celluloid ball remains suspended on the jet of water, that is hardly any time at all. Not that one notices its cessation : the first thing noticed is very often a desire to change the position of the body ; this may draw attention to the fact that for some relatively considerable period of time the mind has been wandering happily down some completely irrelevant by-way of thought. Then, I would suggest, the best thing is to begin again at quiet of body. For those plodding along through the uninteresting desert of the dry prayer of faith, a time of prayer will only too often be a succession of troughs with unimpressive peaks between, the peaks being the sparse and fleeting moments when they have succeeded in what they would regard as praying at all. But, let us remind them, although attention is the specific aim of mental prayer, aimed at as being the means to love, it is the intention that makes an action essentially a prayer, and spending a certain time with the intention of praying is prayer in the sight of God, even if through human frailty attention wavers and is lost ; indeed such a time of prayer may be greatly more valuable before God than a time full of consolation.

The body, then, is an important factor, even in mental prayer. This reflection prompts us to turn to another form of prayer, vocal prayer. It would have been natural to have begun these considerations on prayer with this matter, because after all prayer usually begins with the use of words ; we " say our prayers " long before we are capable of conceiving that there is such a thing as mental prayer. But we also continue to " say our

65

prayers ", and to take part in corporate prayer, which is of necessity vocal, long after we have progressed in mental prayer, in fact always, all through life. So, for the reason given already, I have preferred to say little about vocal prayer until now, when what is said will be read in the light of what has been said earlier ; thus, while presuming that the reader is already familiar with the practice of vocal prayer I hope that a fresh aspect of it may be given.

XII

VOCAL PRAYER

AFTER the Holy Sacrifice of the Mass (in which the utterance of vocal prayer is an integral constituent) the most solemn, majestic and powerful form of Christian prayer is the corporate prayer of the Church, the liturgical office, performed officially in the name of the whole Church, by appointed ministers, and as a grave duty by those in sacred orders. This prayer carries with it the great blessing of Christ "Wherever two or more are gathered together in my name, there am I in the midst of them ". It is corporate—it is the prayer not of isolated souls but of the whole Church as the Body of Christ, and the High Priest who presents it before the throne of the Divine Majesty is none other than the Eternal Word, Jesus Christ Our Lord, through whom we pray. Now this corporate prayer is necessarily, in the nature of things, vocal prayer, the prayer of words, for by no other means than words is it practicable for us to achieve prayer in union with each other. When we seek to pray together, we say prayers together. The first and funda- mental value of such prayer is that it is in the nature of an action, a thing done, a deed acquiring its worth from the intention that directs it. On this point we dwelt a little previously, noting that while it was highly desirable that attention should accompany intention in the performance of the duties of vocal prayer, it was nevertheless as an external action that the duty was directly imposed. A priest has for instance to *say* Office ; the Church knows well that few priests can say it all without distractions and with unflagging attention. Yet while corporate and liturgical prayer is in the first place an action, this does not mean that the accompanying attention is merely a sort of overflow, an additional circumstance which adds to the perfection of the thing done but is not required with any urgency. It is not with vocal prayer as it is with a soldier on parade : the soldier will satisfy all requirements if he performs accurately and smartly the movements commanded him, and no one would dream of inquiring into the thoughts that pass through his mind while he is doing them ; the movements of military ceremonial are not intended to direct his thoughts ; but the movements of liturgical ceremonial, and more particularly the words of vocal prayer, are definitely intended to direct the thoughts of the worshippers, and interior attention, so far as it lies within volitional control, is an integral part of the worship we offer to God. The prayer of words is meant to raise the mind to God, and it is from this point of view, thinking of it in particular as the intended beginning of mental prayer, that these pages are concerned with it. Words, the warp and woof of speech, are chosen as the obviously fitting medium of corporate prayer, not simply because they provide an action in which a body of persons can by uttering or hearing them take their share, but because they are the most natural and simple instrument for arousing thoughts in the mind. That is where prayer ordinarily begins ; when the Apostles asked Our Lord to teach them how to pray He gave them in response the words of the *Our Father*, and if He warned them against the " much speaking " of the heathens[17] it was not against words as the vehicle of prayer that He warned them, but against empty verbiage, divorced from

67

interior attention and sincerity. This however sharpens the point of a difficulty with which we are concerned; for to many, and those not always non-Catholics, the vocal prayer of the Church appears so often to be dissociated from accompanying thought; they are puzzled by the use of a dead language, unintelligible to the majority of the faithful, as the language of the liturgy, and they are scandalised by the placid way in which the Church has so long used a Latin version of the Psalms which not only fails in parts to give the meaning of the Hebrew, but even fails at times to give any intelligible meaning at all; they wonder why it should be desirable to recite psalms which at the moment of recital have no appropriateness whatever to the emotional and mental state of the reciter. But let us begin at the beginning.

The use of words, the saying of prayers, is the natural beginning of prayer. Little children are taught to say their prayers. At this stage the purpose of the words is primarily to introduce thoughts into the mind; and for that painful operation, getting ideas into human heads, there is no shoe-horn more apt and practicable than language. We use set prayers to give expression to thoughts which we would like to have, and the very giving of expression to them puts the thoughts before our minds. This purpose persists throughout life, and the Church has treasures of admirable prayers to meet our every need.

But as our intimacy with Our Lord grows we experience another need: we have thoughts, what we need is to utter them, not in set phrases but in our personal way, and so prayer becomes as St. Teresa puts it ' familiar conversation with Him whom we love '. We speak with Our Lord concerning our interests, cares and anxieties, hopes and desires; we tell Him of those we would like to help, and of how we need His help. Concerning this personal prayer the Holy Father writes in the encyclical on the Mystical Body :—

There are some, moreover, who deny to our prayers of petition any real efficacy, or who suggest that private prayers to God are to be accounted of little value, inasmuch as it is rather the public prayers offered in the name of the Church which have real worth, since they proceed from the mystical Body of Jesus Christ. This suggestion is quite untrue. For the Divine Redeemer holds in close union with Himself not only His Church, as His beloved Bride, but in her also the souls of each one of the faithful, with whom He ardently desires to have intimate converse, especially after they have received Holy Communion. And although public prayer, as proceeding from Mother Church herself, excels beyond any other by reason of the dignity of the Bride of Christ, nevertheless all prayers, even those said in the most private way, have their dignity and their efficacy, and are also of great benefit to the whole mystical Body for in that Body there can be no good and virtuous deed performed by individual members which does not, through the Communion of Saints, redound also to the welfare of all. Nor is it wrong for individuals, simply because they are members of this Body, to ask special favours for themselves, even temporal favours, subject to conformity with the will of God; they are still individual persons, and still subject to their own particular needs.[18]

In such intimate converse as this with the Divine Guest we tell Him also how we love Him, and of our sorrow for sin and eagerness to grow in holiness. We talk to Him of anything and everything that can be a bond of union between us.

Now it is usually when someone is genuinely eager to grow in holiness, and the limitations of such familiar conversation begin to make themselves felt—especially in that it tends inevitably to bring our thoughts back upon ourselves and teaches us little about God Himself

69

—that the need for a richer mental prayer is perceived. Circumstances may favour the person who feels this, and there may be at hand for the taking instruction in the practice of meditation, whether it be derived from the written word or from a living guide. But the Church, a solicitous mother, has provided a means of reaching a fuller mental prayer, meditative and nourishing to the mind, for the countless millions of her children who have not learnt to read, or have no books on prayer at hand, and no director to guide them; it is a means that links the practice of vocal prayer with meditation, and it is a form of prayer which when fully understood is the answer to the difficulty with which we are at the moment concerned, namely that so much of the vocal prayer of the Church appears to the outside critic to be with difficulty distinguished from gabbling or 'vain repetition'. The outstanding example of this prayer is the rosary.

"*Est autem rosarium certa precandi formula, qua quindecim angelicarum salutationum, oratione Dominica interjecta, distinguimus, et ad earum singulas totidem nostrae reparationis mysteria, pia meditatione recolimus.*" "The Rosary is a fixed form of prayer, in which we tell fifteen decades of *Hail Marys*, with an *Our Father* between them, and at each of them recall to mind with devout attention one of fifteen sacred truths concerning our restoration to grace." So does the Church define the rosary in the Roman breviary.[19]

Here therefore is a new use of words in prayer; new in the sense that we have not yet considered it here. The words themselves, the *Our Fathers* and *Hail Marys*, are not the focus of attention; their literal meaning is not the idea we are seeking to introduce into our minds; nor are these words intended to be the expression of ideas present in our minds and to which we seek to give utterance. What then are the words meant to be? What function are they meant to fulfil? The focus of attention is evidently the sacred truth, the mystery, announced

70

for each decade. The actual recitation of the words is presumed to be so familiar and so habitual as to absorb practically no attention at all. Why say them?

This is an objection voiced again and again by bewildered Protestants and even occasionally by Catholics. Now there can be no doubt at all that the Catholic practice of saying the rosary has the full and enthusiastic sanction of the Church. Our Lady herself, in such apparitions as those to St. Bernadette at Lourdes has made it lucidly plain that she wants the rosary said, that it is not a survival from mediæval times but a living reality for to-day. For those therefore who experience the difficulty alluded to, it is worth while giving a word of explanation. Why do we repeat *Hail Marys*, whether collectively or privately, if what we are trying to do is to meditate on the mysteries of our redemption?

The answer is that we can say *Hail Marys* in common together but we cannot meditate in common; the public rosary evidently serves as a bond of union between those who wish to pray together, and anyone who has studied human nature enough to know how difficult it is to get folk even to fill in a ration book correctly will realise that a prayer has to be very simple and very constant if it is to be a successful means to help to pray together. But the answer goes further than that; it is also that many people could not sustain a continuous meditation for any length of time if they had not some thread of occupation to link it with; the saying of the decades provides such a thread of occupation, which absorbs the subliminal attention, and affords a connection which keeps the thoughts together, while before the conscious mind thoughts—not formulated in words, but rich in content—gather and grow; the mind is educated by this devout recalling of the majestic truths.

There have been saints—the Jesuit lay brother St. Alphonsus Rodriguez was one—for whom the recitation of the rosary was an almost ceaseless occupation. Their minds—for they were often souls far advanced in

71

mystical prayer—were surely steeped to their fullest capacity in the intellectual perception of Christian truth ; how could they continue so tirelessly to meditate ? The explanation that suggests itself, in the light of what we have said earlier, is that the rosary itself, the rhythmic sequence of *Paters* and *Aves*, became for them the ' contact ' lifting the consciousness into the supernatural awareness of God, into the enjoyment of that delight which alone of all delights can never sate and cloy. It would not be contrary to the spirit and intention of the Church if in saying the rosary we did not precisely make a discursive meditation on the mystery, but following the attraction of grace as manifested in times of prayer other than the rosary, occupied our attention with the awareness of the presence of God. For those especially who find that there is an increasing difficulty in meditating on the mystery, which in earlier years they had not noticed, this combining of the recitation of the formula with a simplified attention to God may relieve a strain that is becoming intolerable ; the rosary is the poor man's office, and no one who has seen the devout absorption of holy persons saying it can doubt that it is a simple door to the highest forms of prayer.

But there are others who would say that they did not find that the recitation provided for them a means of this profounder recollection, while what they did find was that instead of helping meditation (which without it they could achieve) it seemed rather to hinder a connected sequence of thoughts, and even to make distractions more than ever irresistible. It would be interesting to study statistically the suggestion that these are persons who by education or natural bent are very articulate in their thoughts, that is to say, when they think they at once and automatically put their thoughts into definite expression in words, and are incapable of thinking clearly without this articulate expression. In such a case it would be intelligible that the effort to repeat the formula and at the same time to meditate would result in a sort

72

of interference. Such people would probably notice on the other hand that the automatic recitation of the formula did not seem to interfere at all with involuntary distractions, even though these also were definitely articulate in words; the explanation might be sought in the fact that they are involuntary, that they run, as all distractions do, on their own momentum. It is the effort to guide and control a meditation which is felt to be in conflict with the recitation of the words. Be this as it may, the rosary is Our Lady's special wish; it may be a toil; it may be something of a penance; it will at least be a safeguard against spiritual highbrowism for those who are inclined to fancy themselves above it. It is a prayer that we ought to cling to at all costs. Those who experience the difficulty here mentioned will perhaps be well advised to give more attention than they would have thought necessary to the actual recitation of the words themselves, and at the same time to seek not so much a discursive consideration of the mystery as that simpler sense of the presence of God to which the rosary devoutly said so often leads.[20]

Here we might repeat the suggestion about quiet as the necessary preliminary for prayer. How can we expect the rosary to help us if we plunge into it without recollecting ourselves and are well on our way, somewhat anxious to get to the end, before we have fully recalled to mind what it is that we are doing. Père de Grandmaison cites St. Peter of Alcantara for the view that even if a quarter of an hour, or half an hour, out of an hour's meditation, were spent on securing quiet, it would be time well spent.[21] No less for vocal prayer is quiet needed at the beginning.[22]

The idea of the rosary as a form of vocal prayer deliberately intended to be—as far as the element of words is concerned—rather an accompaniment of other activities of the soul than as a use of language to focus attention and introduce thoughts into the mind, throws light upon that matter previously hinted at. It explains why

Catholics are not as a rule perturbed by having a dead language which they cannot speak as the language of their liturgy ; on the whole they prefer it. It explains the placid acceptance of the Vulgate version of the Psalms in the office, and the unruffled calm with which the users of the breviary recite sacred poems which have no relation to their personal feelings at the time. For Catholics, unlike some types of Nonconformist, do not feel their prayers to be bursts of oratory, however sacred. They feel them to be far more acts of worship. If the verbal content of the prayers be rather removed from their personal state of mind at the moment, that is no tragedy, for Catholic prayer is above all corporate ; it is the prayer of the Body of Christ, in union with the Head, and in its magnificent perspectives small personal interests dwindle and grow insignificant.

One broad effect of the Protestant movement was to fix the minds of men on man, and to cramp them even further into the narrow circle of the self, the ego ; this in part is the cause of that impatience which finds a source of irritation in the impersonal note of Catholic prayer. And the Protestant movement which broke the statues, smashed the stained-glass windows and threw down the altars, making paving-stones of the stones which had been consecrated for the sacramental sacrifice, made the pulpit the effectually predominant centre of the church ; hence it made the spoken word, as the vehicle of intelligible thought, assume an importance it had not had in Christian worship. Language, as an instrument of worship, was impoverished by its restriction to prosaic rational uses. But the Church knows human nature better than that, and not only does She in her worship make the fullest use of music and of stately ritual, of light and colour and fragrance, and of all that can be charged with a symbolism and a significance too rich for words, but She knows also that words themselves are capable of more than the expression of dictionary meanings. She knows not only the importance of the body as a factor

74

in prayer, but the inexhaustible potentialities of language, no less than of other things, for lifting the mind and heart to God. Hence if we find such Catholic practices as the saying of the rosary and the use of Latin jarring to our sensibilities, it will be well for us to pause and speculate whether the fault does not lie in our own pedestrian characteristics.

But words have another close relation to mental prayer : the saying of prayers is the natural beginning of prayer, for words are the carriers of ideas ; they bring ideas to the mind. They offer therefore an easy bridge to discursive meditation when they are used in the manner, already alluded to, which St. Ignatius puts forward as the second of three additional ways of prayer, supplementary to the methods proposed in the text of the *Exercises*. A word is a carrier of an idea, and one idea may evoke many others. He suggests this simple device, that we should take one by one the words of a prayer, for example the *Our Father*, and draw from each word the fullest train of thought that it can inspire. " The Way of Perfection " of St. Teresa is one splendid illustration of the inexhaustible wealth of the best of all prayers, used thus as a mine for the delvings of discursive meditation.

St. Ignatius in his ' Third Method ' makes another suggestion which, like many of his masterly hints on prayer, seems to envisage the leading of the souls beyond the intellectual scope of discursive meditation. He suggests that using the words of some prayer, as in the ' Second Method ', we should vary the activity by not following the thoughts evoked by each word to their full run, but passing slowly and evenly from one word to the next, timing the rhythm by letting a breath come between each pair of words. It is difficult to resist the conclusion that he was aiming at a kind of prayer in which there was less intellectual activity, and that he was preparing the way for a simple absorption in the presence of God by proposing a use of words in prayer not unlike the use we have just been discussing in connection with the rosary, namely using words more as an accompaniment to recollection than as a stimulus to reasoning.

A similar trait in his guidance in prayer may be observed in another place. This too reveals his sensitive appreciation of the part played in prayer by the body, for it is to the body particularly that the " senses of the imagination " pertain. St. Ignatius is copiously insistent in the earlier ' contemplations ' of the Exercises, on an elaborate apparatus of imaginative evocation, as an aid to prayerful thought. He stresses the desirability of vivid exactness in " seeing the spot ". Yet there is no doubt that he means the picturing of a scene as a prelude to intellectual activity, not as an end in itself. He would have had little pity for the legendary novice who spent his hour's meditation composing a ' Bethlehem ' only to discover with chagrin at the last moment that he had put St. Joseph in a draught. The Ignatian ' composition of place ' is meant as a prelude to thought. What then can be the reason why later in the day St. Ignatius proposes a form of meditation which seems intended to steep the consciousness more in sense-impressions than in discursive reasoning ? That the sense-impressions in question are evocations through memory, and not direct impressions from material objects, does not affect the issue. St. Ignatius emphatically distinguishes this new form of meditation from the ' contemplation ' (his name for imaginative meditation) by giving it a special name —" application of the senses "—or at least by employing the phrase rendered in the literal Latin version of his autograph as "*trahere sensus super contemplationem*" (to draw the senses over the contemplation).

It may be that he proposed this as an occupation in prayer for the evening of a fatiguing day in which four exercises of an hour apiece had already been performed, judging that it would be something of a relaxation and a change. What he proposes is that with the scene (pictured in the preceding exercises) before the mind, we should first look, and then listen, and then use the other senses, adding that from those separate absorptions in sense-impressions we should " draw some fruit "—the phrase seems studiously vague. Surely St. Ignatius was deliberately opening the door to simple absorption in the supernatural awareness of God. He was human enough, and poet enough, to know the tranquillising effect of a quiet looking and listening, in which the restless analytic intellect is stilled ; and who can doubt that he saw or learnt from experience that a similar tranquillity in mental prayer is an apt overture for the far faint music of the voice of God singing to the soul. He provides the link himself, for when he speaks of the senses of taste and smell—those senses so recalcitrant to æsthetic sublimation—what he proposes is that we should smell and taste the infinite sweetness (*suavitatem ac dulcedinem*) of the Divinity, of the soul, of its virtues and of other things according to the special character (*rationem*) of the person we are contemplating.[23]

Here then again, it seems to me, St. Ignatius reveals not only the sensitive adaptability of his teaching in prayer, and the manifold variety it presents to meet the manifold variety of individual development in different souls, but also his penetrating intuitions into the inter-relations of soul and body, imagination and intellect, nature and super-nature, in the marvellous world of prayer.

These remarks concerning the prayer of words, with the above hark-back to the use of the imagination in prayer, have been set, with full animadvertence to their placing, after a passage on the rule of the body in prayer. The purpose was this : there is a discernible tendency towards a division of taste or opinion concerning prayer ; the passage cited earlier from the Encyclical *Mystici Corporis Christi* is evidence enough ; some are inclined to regard private interior prayer—with an emphasis on the name contemplation—as the great thing, and to feel exterior or vocal prayer as an interruption ; others more liturgical in their enthusiasm are on the contrary prone to consider private prayer, and meditation in particular, as a somewhat donnish preoccupation, akin to the potterings of scholarship, a little academic and unreal, and a not altogether warrantable subtraction from the time that might be given to the real business of chanting (or reciting) the praises of God. The purpose of the present correlation of vocal prayer and the influence of the body in prayer, and the juxtaposition of them near a context concerned with the evolution of simple supernatural prayer out of intellectual formation, is to emphasise the unity of the whole. Christian prayer is one thing; it is the homecoming of creature to Creator. If there are many ways home it is because those coming home are many, and are luxuriantly diverse in their qualities and characteristics. The purpose of this emphasis on the unity is also to encourage those whose practical experience of prayer has been largely confined to the patient saying of prayers, and who may feel that the subtleties and complications touched on in these pages, and all the paraphernalia of methodic meditation, are things that have no relation to their homely, busy lives. It is to assure them that their simple way—their devout persistence in the rosary for example—can lead, no less surely than the most erudite instruction in methods of prayer, to a deep supernatural awareness of God. "Of him to whom much is given, much shall be required": where there are gifts of intellect and education, a profound formation of mind through mental prayer may be exacted by the Holy Spirit; but for all that it has pleased Our Father to hide many things from the wise and prudent and reveal them to little ones. No one is excluded from the invitation to the deepest prayer by reason of a mere dearth of intellectual culture. Yet on the other hand not only does the Catechism say of meditation that it is useful to make it daily, for such was the practice of all the saints, but the Holy Father continues the passage cited above with the words: "As for

78

meditation on heavenly things, not only the pronounce-
ments of the Church but also the practice and example
of the saints are a proof of the high estimation in which
it must be held by all." There are many ways of prayer,
but all the ways lead home, and all are meant to converge
on that supernatural gift which is faith, and which is
the central topic of this book.

To that topic, therefore, to the Prayer of Faith,[24] as
here understood, let us return. But first let us add a
last remark bearing on the relation of words in prayer
to the development of supernatural awareness of God.
The question is simply this : granting that to pray by
saying prayers is an excellent thing in itself, is it likely
that there will come a time when it is better to diminish
the number of prayers we use ? Notice that this is not
quite the same as another question : is it better when
praying to go over in detail, by name and special
circumstance, the persons or intentions we wish to pray
for, or to leave the details to our guardian angel, and
devote our attention to God ? To this subsidiary question I would answer : if you can pray best by remember-
ing this ' shopping-list ' of daily bread, do so ; use the
details so long as they are a help ; but as soon as you
find that in prayer you can forget creatures and fix your
thoughts on God, cram the shopping-list into the hands
of St. Joseph or somebody and turn your thoughts wholly
to God Himself ; ' Think of Me and I will think of you ',
He said to one of His friends ; we cannot ensure the
filling of our spiritual shopping-basket better than by
thus handing it over to God's care ; the adoration of
radiant trust and love is far more powerful with God
than the pre-occupation of human solicitude. But this
was a subsidiary question ; the first one raised was
whether it is likely to become better to diminish the
number of our vocal prayers or to persevere in saying
them ? St. Thomas Aquinas gives the answer : "*In
singulari oratione tantum est vocibus, et hujusmodi signis,
utendum, quantum proficit ad excitandum interius mentem : si*

vero mens per hoc distrahatur, vel qualitercumque impediatur, est a talibus cessandum : quod praecipue contingit in his, quorum mens sine hujusmodi signis est sufficienter ad devotionem parata." ("Then alone should we use words and such like signs when they help to excite the mind internally. But if they distract or in any way impede the mind we should abstain from them ; and this happens chiefly to those whose mind is sufficiently prepared for devotion without having recourse to those signs.")[25]

In the first place let us note that the answer applies to individual or private prayer. (That this is the meaning of *singulari oratione* is clear from the rest of the context. The 'alone' of the translation cited does not quite convey the force of this.) All prayers of duty are primarily external actions, and only in the extremest cases should they be omitted because of difficulty arising from interior conditions of prayer. An example of an extreme case might be St. Ignatius, exempted from saying the Office because he was so carried away by the fervour to which it gave rise that he could never finish it within reasonable time.

Secondly St. Thomas's answer makes it plain that the very means used at the commencement of prayer to arouse in our minds an awareness of God can, in the progress of the evolution of prayer, become a hindrance to that awareness. This fits in quite easily with what we have been saying : growth in prayer is normally the emergence into conscious use of powers that are supernatural, and this involves a new aiming or focusing of the centre of attention ; it may well happen that a division of attention between the lower operation of reciting vocal prayers and the higher operation of grasping supernaturally the presence of God, will lead to a sense of tension or struggle that interferes with both. In such a condition voluntary private vocal prayer should be curtailed.[26]

Nor is it needful to wait till there is a pronounced sense of conflict. The words are means ; the awareness of God is the end. We may lawfully diminish vocal prayer simply to be more ready for supernatural attention to God, even when that is not an activity that is being imposed upon us but one that we are trying to reach.[27]

In practice, therefore, the guiding rule is to be as docile as possible to the impulses of grace, and to avoid both lagging back or resisting, as much as we avoid racing ahead.

" *Vocibus et hujusmodi signis*," says St. Thomas, " words and suchlike signs". The use of imaginative scenes is subject to the same rule. If they should prove to be a hindrance rather than a help to " devotion "—by which the mind of the person praying is raised up to God, St. Thomas adds by way of explanatory comment—then they should be dispensed with. In short the principle is that as long as a natural operation facilitates the action of grace it is to be used; when it interferes it is to be discontinued.

XIII

THE PRAYER OF FAITH

" THE PRAYER OF FAITH " is the title chosen for this book. The reason for concentrating attention on this kind of prayer is that it seems to be the characteristic prayer of most people who are striving to lead lives of prayer, in our times at least, and to remain so for the greater part of those lives. Let us now try to sum up what has been said about it.

Though it has been necessary to insist that a life of prayer is a growth, and as such is bound to go through phases or stages which differ from each other, we have of set purpose endeavoured to avoid making sharp outlines for the various phases, and have very carefully abstained from giving names to them. It is usual to do so in books about prayer; authors vie with each other in the length of their lists of names ; they appear eager to set milestones along the way. That this is not done here is partly due to the conviction that such meticulous surveying only stimulates in readers an unprofitable anxiety to recognise the milestones ; and partly—chiefly in fact—to the conviction that as generalised statements applied to all persons the marking off of stages becomes false. For preference we have suggested an image that makes the divisions vertically instead of horizontally, along instead of across : the development of prayer is not like a rope consisting of separate lengths of different colours, it is like a rope woven of strands of different colours ; and though at this stage or at that, in this soul or in that, one might say that the rope was of a certain colour, this would only be because at that stage the strands of that colour predominated ; it would not be because the strands of other colours were absent altogether. And the processes by which at different times different colours predominate are very gradual processes, so that the colours merge very considerably into each other, and they are processes extremely unpredictable in their occurrence. No two souls are alike, not more in prayer than anywhere else.

In attempting therefore to give a clear explanation of what is here meant by the Prayer of Faith, it is our studied intention to avoid giving the impression that it is one sharply outlined stretch of the way of prayer.

The Prayer of Faith is a supernatural activity. But saying this is not telling us much. All Christian prayer is supernatural. It is all enlivened by divine charity and is the activity of supernaturalised souls—or else it is not Christian prayer at all. By the Prayer of Faith we mean a raising of the soul to God in which the knowledge or thought-factor is not merely supernaturalised but is experienced as such. It is a communion with God in which the soul is aware of His reality and of His presence by a sort of ' sixth-sense ' or ' second-sight ' or ' telepathy ' which is specifically different from the kind of certainty that He exists attained by logical demonstration. It is a certainty different also from the assent of faith given by Christians in everyday conditions; but it differs from this not specifically, but only because that same certainty of faith has moved, so to speak, into the sensitive focus of consciousness. Hence there is no sharp break in the development of this prayer out of the less experiential 'acts of faith' with which the prayer of Christians ordinarily begins. There is instead an imperceptible brightening and intensifying of the soul's assurance that God is there, until it becomes a knowledge immediate and direct, resembling in immediacy the knowledge given by the senses. The soul 'feels' aware of God's presence, as the eye is aware of light and of objects visible in the light. It was to suggest this immediacy as well as the supernatural character of the knowledge that we used the expressions like 'sixth-sense' above; not of course intending them to be read literally.

Readers acquainted with the literature of mystical theology will have recognised (as was previously noted in these pages) that this sense of the presence of God is traditionally regarded as the essential mark of the mystical states. Are we therefore to say that the prayer which is the main topic of this book is mystical prayer? It seems to me an unprofitable question for a book intended for the general reader; doubtless it is of importance for experts, but it is no concern of people who just want to reach God through prayer. " I would rather feel compunction," says Thomas à Kempis, " than know its definition ". A similar frame of mind with regard to the gifts of prayer is much to be desired. So too the practice of giving marks by which the advent of mystical graces may be diagnosed does not seem to me profitable for the general reader, but only provocative of a self-consciousness and a self-analysis that will probably do as much to damp the mystical powder as it will to load the gun. In any case the marks are never very informative except to those who, looking back from the skyline of ascent in prayer, no longer need the information. For instance[28] it is said that mystical prayer does not depend on our will, cannot be foreseen, often stops suddenly and cannot be stopped at will. But anyone who has tried to write a story or a poem—or even an essay at school—knows that much the same phraseology might be used with reference to literary ' inspiration '. It might even be applied quite sincerely to the kind of ' inspiration ' that makes a man a superlative golfer on one glorious day, while the rest of the year he is a rabbit. The subjective impression that it is not ourselves who are praying—so much are we apparently carried by a force within us—is no very reliable sign of mystical graces ; it could be confused by a beginner who has no actual experience of those graces, with the sort of facility felt when a story ' writes itself ' or an essay ' just comes '. And the beginner is just the person who matters in this connection. And conversely the absence of this subjective impression, the opposite feeling that we are doing the praying, is no proof that the special experimental awareness of God is absent. The fact is that it is as difficult, and as profitless, for a soul growing in prayer to calculate where it stands, as it is for a young girl to know " whether this is really love ". If it is, you will know ; if it is not, a book full of symptoms will only make you think it is.

We need not therefore enter into the question whether the Prayer of Faith, as here understood, is a mystical state or not. My own opinion is that theoretically the paths of prayer can be described as passing along three levels, the valley, the hillsides and the crest of the ridge : in the valley there is faith simply ; on the hillsides that faith has strengthened into experiential awareness of the fact *that* God exists ; on the hill crest there is knowledge direct and supernatural of *what* God is (a knowledge quite impossible to confuse with the knowledge of what God is obtained by studying the catechism). I should prefer to reserve the term mystical for paths passing along the ridge. This book is concerned chiefly with the hillside. It is addressed principally to people keeping up a habit of spending time regularly in mental prayer, and who find themselves discouraged because they seem to be getting nowhere. Its main point is that they are really getting on very well, that there is normally a long phase in the life of prayer which has just this look of futility and lack of progress, and it should not cause discouragement.

This long phase we have named the Prayer of Faith. It is substantially the same thing as what St. John of the Cross calls the Night of Sense, the first part of the Dark Night of the Soul. If it differs from that, the difference lies rather in the persons concerned than in the state. St. John is speaking to those whom the Holy Spirit wishes to lead on to the ridge. He envisages the Night of Sense as a relatively short prelude. He is in something of a hurry to get through the description of it and get on to the mystical prayer to which he sees it as leading. Now it would seem, whatever the reason, that among the many who persevere in mental prayer in these days, a great proportion are destined to walk most of their lives along the sloping hillsides. The Prayer of Faith is their appointed lot it seems. To such especially these pages are addressed.

It is not part of our aim to discuss the vexed question whether or not all Christians who devote themselves to mental prayer are meant by the Holy Spirit to reach the ridge. If one tries to settle the issue by appeal to the authority of writers, opinions will be found to be fairly evenly divided. Big guns fire on both sides. Some tell you that becoming a mystic is easy and that everyone ought to become one. Others tell you that it is outrageous presumption to think of such a thing, at least for the likes of you. All agree that mystical prayer is an absolutely free gift of God and nothing that we can do will automatically bring us to it; all we can do is to prepare the way. All agree that mystical graces are not the same thing as holiness; all admit that they are a great help to holiness; lively discussion centres round the question whether one can become a great saint without them. Whatever may be the answers to these questions, most of us are plodding doggedly along the hillside and the special aim of these pages is to comfort those who are.

The Prayer of Faith then corresponds generally to the Night of Sense. Perhaps the greatest debt that Christianity owes to St. John of the Cross is for the clarity with which he showed that the Dark Night of the Soul was not a dead loss in the spiritual life, or at best a punishment of sin, to be borne with patience and humility, but was an integral part of the development of prayer. It is this clue we are following now. In everyday practice few things are more necessary than this conviction; it is surprisingly difficult to convince people that the fact that their prayer is dry and without consolation is not a proof that Our Lord is angry with them for some fault they cannot put their finger on.

Like the Night of Sense the Prayer of Faith has two sides to it, a positive and a negative constituent. The positive constituent is the experiential awareness of the presence of God. The negative constituent is the slowing down or interference perceived in the activities of intellect or imagination which were, to begin with, the most noticeable activities in mental prayer. What we have been trying to show is that the two constituents are connected, that the negative one appears simply in order that the positive one may be strengthened. In fact all that kind of jamming that supervenes in the human faculties—up to and including the extraordinary paralysis which is called ecstasy, in which the soul completely ceases to exert normal control over the body—is due to a process of readjustment by which the human consciousness adapts itself to the supernatural mode of knowledge.

Now it is important to observe that in the positive

constituent the experiential awareness of the presence of God, there is in operation the same law of up-and-down, ebb and flow, night and day, as we noted in other phases of prayer. That was one reason for choosing the name Prayer of Faith, in preference to St. John's Night of Sense; to underline a fact which St. John himself makes quite clear, but which by reason of the associations of the word 'Night' many are apt to miss: namely that the Night of Sense is a night as far as the use of natural faculties is concerned, but is a varying and alternating night and day as far as the special element of awareness of God is concerned.

We began this explanation by describing the desert or darkness at a moment of 'ebb' or 'down'. Now we have to stress that it is not all ebb; there is also flow.

The Prayer of Faith has its night and its day. The day is the enjoyment of that inexplicable sense of the presence of God; the night is the sense of His absence. By 'sense' we mean a subjective impression, something we feel. It does not in the least mean that God is more present to us when we feel He is near us, or more absent when we feel Him absent. This reality of His presence has nothing to do directly with our feeling. The reality depends on whether we sin or not. The state of awareness we are in, is not a measure of the closeness of God to us in actuality. It is simply an instrument He uses to elicit from our wills the substantial love of Himself, and it works just as well—perhaps better—for that purpose when it is an 'awareness of absence' as when it is an 'awareness of presence'. For this fluctuating subjective condition is only the measure of how much the gift of supernatural knowledge is at any moment affecting our consciousness; it is not the measure of how great a power of loving God we have acquired through the life of grace. There is a difference between the amount of learning a man has absorbed, and the amount of it which at any given moment is present to his consciousness or readily available, and there is a great difference between the union with God that a soul has attained and the conscious awareness of it that the person experiences.

There will, therefore, be ups and downs, fluctuations in the intensity of the sense of the presence of God. What the causes of these fluctuations may be in any given instance it passes the wit of man to say. Since the awareness itself is something supernatural one is predisposed to conclude that fluctuations in it must be due to the action of God directly ; but on the other hand so sweetly and so delicately does the Holy Spirit accommodate His action to the creatures of His power, that one is equally inclined to allow much for conditions in the person affecting the state of prayer. Such physical conditions as fatigue or illness seem often to play a part. Much more noticeably changes in the moral temperature, such as dissipation or deliberate imperfection, to say nothing of sin, are seen to affect the prayer. But it is not possible, and it is not necessary, to know just why God withdraws this consolation at any given moment. What is necessary is to respond rightly to the change, and this brings in the whole important matter of indifference, with which we shall deal presently.

As outlined earlier, the progressive development of this Prayer of Faith is accompanied by a progressive whittling away of the merely natural activities. In fact what we mean by the Prayer of Faith is a prayer in which those things have been whittled away to almost nothing, and there is left just the bare faith—either in consolation when God seems indescribably close, or in desolation when He seems agonisingly absent. But the impression aimed at in that outline was one of great variety or variation, as between one soul and another, in this lessening or simplifying of intellectual or imaginative activity. For many there may be a very full development of the supernatural ' taste ' or ' touch ' of God with a rich accompaniment of natural activity. For others there may be a great dearth of any occupation satisfying to the human faculties, and yet a very faint experience of the supernatural. And these differences may be perceived at separate times by the same person.

So incalculable are the varieties of personal characteristics and histories that no useful composite photographs of these things can be made. It would seem that those of active imagination and lively emotion are more disposed to accompany the sense of the presence of God with thoughts or images, and often to receive much delight and consolation (of a sensible or felt character) through them. Dom Chapman[29] suggests that the 'obscure contemplation' (he is speaking of what we have called awareness of the presence) does in imaginative persons 'translate' itself into 'phantasmata' and the imagination and emotions may be full of joy. Such 'translation' would in practice be indistinguishable from the rising up into the field of consciousness of ideas previously stored in the mind and now illuminated by a special radiance coming from the soul's enjoyment of God as present. There is nothing to be gained by tracing the source of the ideas or images so aroused. The important thing is to know what to do about them. Apart from the safeguard we proposed some pages back —that is testing the ideas by the teaching of the Church and accepting them on the ground that they really come through that unimpeachable channel—the best thing to do about them is to take them when they come, and not strain to produce them when they do not.[30]

It is well known that St. John of the Cross counsels the avoiding in prayer of " all visible and bodily things for they are a hindrance in our way ", exception made, a little inconsistently, for the Humanity of Our Lord. St. Teresa, on the other hand, declares that " to withdraw the thoughts from all corporeal things like the angelic spirits who are always inflamed with love is not possible for us while in this mortal flesh ".[31] We need not quarrel with her implied assertion that the angels would have imaginations if they were not so inflamed with love, because this would be irrelevant if not irreverent. What we should notice is that these two great ' doctors ' differ. The difference appears a personal one. For ourselves we must find what helps us. It is tempting to speculate that the underlying reason for St. John's uncompromising rejection of imagination—and for the matter of that of discursive reason—is that what suited him best as the ' carrier ' for supernatural knowledge was a purely intellectual contemplation, angelic in kind rather than normally human (and quite beyond the reach of the valiant woman of Avila), and that this contemplation is what ' natural mystics ' like neo-Platonists have in mind when they speak of mysticism. But this would take us into waters too deep for our present purpose.[32] The practical note is—if St. John's writings help you, use them ; but do not strain to do exactly what he recommends in every detail, because it may not suit your spiritual make-up. You may safely stretch your powers trying to live up to all he says about moral purgation and getting rid of sin.

An excellent description of the prayer of which we are speaking is given in " The Cloud of Unknowing ".[33]

XIV

SOME ADVANTAGES

BROADLY speaking we may say that the way in which this Prayer of Faith strikes ordinary folk who come to it is as something rather unimpressive. The prevailing impression is given in the phrase " I am doing nothing ". There is a general sense of untidiness. Nothing seems to be happening. There are moments of intenser consolation, but they are few. In good times there is a sense of peace and contentment, a satisfaction in being at prayer which appears difficult to explain, since there is seemingly nothing to account for the satisfaction. In the lean years prayer is distressing because it appears such a waste of time—nothing but an unavailing effort to chase a clutter of hens out of the flower-garden, throwing stones with one hand, as it were, at pertinacious distractions, and groping with the other for someone or something, in the dark. Underlying this confused and unsatisfactory state of mind there is, as we have been trying to explain, the fundamental fact that this prayer consists essentially—as regards the factor of knowledge which enters into it—of the gradual emergence of a supernatural mode of knowledge. Precisely because it is supernatural it gives no satisfaction to the powers previously utilised in presenting matter to consciousness. And it is to prevent those powers, and the interesting matter they present, from absorbing the attention, that the blankness or darkness descends upon the mind. But it is precisely in the fact that what is given to the mind by this obscure contemplation cannot satisfy the ordinary appetites of the mind that its greatest value lies. For the complementary truth is that this imperceptible nourishment, this invisible light, does not interfere with the ordinary occupations of the mind. True enough, they interfere with it, at first ; and to give it a chance to develop, they are ' blacked out ' during prayer. But it does not interfere with them, and once it has grown strong in the soul it will persist during them. It is like an infra-red ray which the ordinary eyes of the soul cannot see ; but given the apparatus of grace, the soul will come to perceive this ray, without ceasing at the same time to perceive all that the daylight reveals.

It is not possible to combine vocal prayer with commonplace occupation beyond an occasional ejaculation. It is not possible to combine meditation with daily tasks, unless they are routine manual labour of the simplest kind. But the special value of the Prayer of Faith is that just because it is functioning on a different plane, it is quite compatible with other occupations. Hence it is that the lives of the saints are studded with allusions to the fact that their prayer was uninterrupted and continuous. It was certainly not that they were getting eight hundred and fifty-three ejaculations into a common-or-garden five minutes. It was that their souls, by a window of consciousness above the level of ordinary awareness, were unintermittently gazing towards God.

It was doubtless of an advanced development of prayer that the Venerable Marie de l'Incarnation was speaking when she said this, but there is a continuity in prayer: it is the same supernatural life operating all the time, even if there are marked differences in the completeness of its operation; she said: " Since that time my soul has abided in its centre, God. That centre is in itself, and it is there above all consciousness. This is so simple and so delicate a thing that I cannot express it. It is possible to speak of anything, to read, to write, to work, to do all that one wills, without distraction from this occupation and without ceasing to be united to God."[34]

But though that degree is not reached without special grace, it is on that ladder that the soul sets its foot from the moment when it makes a simple act of faith. The rungs are continuous after that. In fully developed cases, as Père Poulain has noted, the prayer persists even during sleep.[35]

Another advantage is that as the supernatural activity does not of itself engage the brain, it is very restful. What weariness accompanies it is due to the toil of the attention resisting distractions, or in happier moments following thoughts that harmonise with the sense of the presence. But when the ' contact ' is very simple, when the awareness of God is revived by a single word or a phrase, and sustained for long periods, then the prayer is almost as refreshing to the nervous system as is sleep. This helps us to understand more readily how it was possible for so many of the saints to work a sixteen-hour day and then spend five or six of the remaining eight hours in prayer.[36]

It is this simple, supernatural prayer which is especially

suited to those leading the mixed life of action and contemplation fused together. The modern trend in religious life has been towards a lessening of the amount of vocal prayer in common, and towards compensating for the absence of the material cloister-wall by an intenser personal detachment ; but this trend has not altered the supernatural essence of Christian prayer. Intensive methodical meditation has taken the place of the diffused but continuous atmosphere of monastic life, simply because intensive meditation is a speedier way of accomplishing the preliminary mental formation, necessary for the emergence of the supernatural gift. But this intellectual preliminary is only a pre-liminary.

It is clearly this prayer, introduced by vigorous mental discipline, that St. Ignatius envisaged as the characteristic prayer of the Jesuit. As is well known, he did not at first consider that the scholastics of the Society would require a daily hour of mental prayer ; he expected them to preserve their interior union with God on a much shorter ration of mental prayer ; doubtless because the early Jesuits were in the main older men, on whom the impact of the Exercises was such that it liberated almost instantaneously the full energy of the supernatural prayer. Experience proved that this was an optimistic estimate of his, and the regular hour of meditation was soon made a part of the rule.[37] But as Père Brou points out : ' Dans L'entourage (de S. Ignace) quand on voulait définir l'oraison propre à la Compagnie, ce n'est pas sur ce que nous appelons méthodes qu'on insistait, mais sur l'esprit, sur la necessité d' harmoniser la prière et la vocation apostolique."[38] Father Nadal writes in the same strain. " The prayer proper to the Society includes both the use of vocal prayer and all the ministries that concern us. It consists in this : that, with the grace of Jesus Christ, enlightenments of the mind, right dispositions in the will, and a union with God (persisting even outside prayer strictly so-called), accompany and guide all our actions in such a way that we find God in all things."[39]

The third and greatest advantage of this Prayer of Faith is its influence upon our conduct. When all is said and done, conduct outside the time of prayer is the real test of prayer. " Blessed are ye if ye shall do these things." In an earlier comment upon prayer that is predominantly affective, we noted that it not only tends to be emotionally exhausting, but that it does not always have a marked effect upon subsequent conduct. Experience will soon show that the dry, almost imperceptible nourishment of the Prayer of Faith even when it is passing through a trough of desolation, strengthens the will and provides force of character to meet the exigencies of real life. For although in this descriptive analysis of what it is, we have almost confined attention to the factor of knowledge or consciousness, it is not that factor which is the vital principle or soul of prayer ; that is only the body of it ; that is only the rope, whose weaving and texture we have been considering ; the pull on the rope is what matters ; the vitality, the life, the soul of all prayer is the love that is achieved through it.

Therefore to complete this account of the Prayer of Faith we must now turn to that other aspect of it. The phases or stages of a life of prayer are distinguished from each other more easily by the changes or differences in the factor of knowledge, but there is likewise a progress in the factor of love. It is rather a question of an increase in strength than of a change in kind ; the pull on the rope remains a pull even though it gets stronger. But there are discernible differences in the character or quality of the love we attain through prayer, and it is of these discernible differences that we are now endeavouring to treat. The fundamental change is not easy to perceive ; it is that change by which our merely human wills are transformed by the pouring forth of the Holy Spirit into our hearts, so that our wills are informed and transformed by divine charity. But this substantial and all-important

94

transformation, taking place from the moment when grace floods the soul, and giving supernatural value to all we do, does not reveal itself in experience until the highest flights of prayer are reached. What we are concerned with at the moment is a double development, discernible sooner. In the first place we are concerned with a less important development, which goes along with the general diminution of natural activity within the sphere of consciousness in prayer ; this less important development is the gradual fading-away of emotional elements in our love. Of this there is not much need to speak ; in practice people do not draw a sharp line between thinking and feeling, between ideas or images and the emotions they arouse ; and all that has been said of the progressive simplification of ideas and imagery can easily be applied to the accompanying affective states. In brief, we grow to love God more but we feel it less. It is this perhaps more than any other phenomenon which prompts us instinctively to use the adjective ' dry ' when adverting to the prayer of faith.

The other important change can be discerned not so much directly in the quality of our love, as in the judgments of value we begin to make, the order in which we come to prize things, the frame of mind we begin to acquire. In a word, as the supernatural sense of God begins to grow, it engenders in our minds judgments of the relative values of things which begin to make us see that God is beyond all relation or proportion to anything and everything else. We really begin to do what we have perhaps long done in words : we begin to put God first, and so completely and sovereignly first that to think of comparing anything with Him would seem more absurd than to compare the length of our little finger with the astronomical immensities of the yet-uncharted universe. But this is only arrived at by beginning at detachment from self. And it is because the Prayer of Faith is so potent a developer of detachment from self that it is such a valuable prayer. We propose

95

now therefore to consider this prayer with that especially in view.

XV

DETACHMENT FROM SELF

GOD, the Creator, is really distinct from His creation; Christians are not pantheists; we do not believe that we are literally God's thoughts, or any kind of ' emanations' from Him, or that there is one totality of being of which we are parts. Between Creator and creature there is a gulf that is infinite. We exist and He exists, but the very word ' being ' has to be understood when it is used of God in a way different from the way in which it is understood when it is applied to creatures. God, the one divine Being, is entirely outside that scale of existence which has for its lowest step inert material things, like sticks and stones, and rises through all gradations of plant and animal life, to the majestic image of God in reasoning man, and beyond him to the towering sublimities of angelic spirits. God is beyond it all, incomprehensible, infinite. Nevertheless so close is He to us that if we said we were His thoughts, meaning that we depend upon His knowledge and will as the creations of an artist proceed from the artist's mind, we should be understating, not overstating, the truth. We are absolutely and entirely dependent on God, to the innermost fibre of our being, to the most secret recesses of our spirit, for every throb of the heart and every flash of thought. There is nothing in all the incommensurable vastness of the cosmos, nothing in the innermost penetralia of our souls, that does not depend immediately and directly upon the ' ground of being and granite of it ' God.

And yet we are free. We have free will. The creative power in whose hands the sidereal spaces and the innumerable galaxies of the solar systems are but a little dust, exerting itself to an achievement which we should have declared impossible and a contradiction in terms if we had been consulted beforehand, has called into existence beings who are free, even while they are entirely dependent. This is a truth to the acceptance of which reason itself should lead but which must remain always, in spite of that acceptance, an impenetrable mystery to reason, an antinomy, a seeming contradiction.

We are not only free. We are self-developing. It is not that we can exist without our environment, or that we can develop ourselves independently of that environment. It is that the power of choice, the free will, governs and controls our development, determining autonomously, in essential measure, the use we make of what our environment provides. We are given a certain starting-point, a constitution, bodily and mental, a history, a matrix of circumstances which holds us at every instant of our existence : yet how we react to that total setting, the use we make of the elements given us for the moulding of our personality, this rests finally with our free will.

We are self-developing, moulding ourselves to a pattern by a series of choices, steering a certain course along a given sea whose waters are astir with currents and cross-currents so complex as to defy analysis. What we are, what we make of ourselves, is the course we steer, and in appraising its worth God will consider not merely the point at which we have arrived, but also the currents and cross-currents, making the complete allowance that only His infinite knowledge can make, for all that has hindered us and made the going hard. This series of choices, the acts of our responsible free will, emerges gradually as we come to the full use of reason, out of a deeper series that remains always submerged below the level of full awareness. But character begins to shape itself almost from the first moments of life, and if the Church does not subject our actions to the tribunal of Penance till we are ' about the age of seven years ', this is not to say that choices made long before, made even in the cradle, do not affect our personality. Hence the grave responsibility of parents who can do so much to guide those choices before the mind itself is fully able to deliberate between alternatives. In this process of self-development we have one great driving-force : it is the vital urge to seek what is ' good ', showing itself from the moment when the baby lungs gasp instinctively for air and the baby lips suck the mother's breast, and showing itself continuously ever after in the innumerable impulses by which we reach out for whatever satisfies us, whatever we need, whatever we feel hunger or desire for. ' Good ' means, in this context, all that is an answer to our cravings, of whatever sort they be.

And in the very nature of things this vital urge which impels us to reach out for ' good ' is a self-centred force ; its purpose and aim is to develop and build up the self of which it is the vital impulse.

Now the first great issue which begins to determine whether a man is going to be a good man or a bad man, is the issue which hangs in the balance when the question arises : is he going to live for himself, with total disregard for others, or is he going to realise that he is not self-sufficient, that others have their vital claims, and that the way to his best self-development lies in seeking not a ' good ' exclusively focused in himself, but the good of the human unity of which he is only one cell.

It is at this point that a man begins to be selfish or unselfish, egoist or altruist. Alas, the beginning of selfishness is often in the pram, long before the small baby can be held responsible for reasoned choices, but at a time when its choices can be guided by the way in which it is treated, when a timely slap or firm handling can check a long series of selfish habits, caught in the toils of which the individual himself may long have to struggle, even with the best of wills to be free from them. Such is the responsibility of parents who control this crucial stage that we can only marvel at God for setting it upon them.

This is the watershed that ultimately determines the flow of the river. According to this interior attitude —whether the person is seeking self inordinately or not —is the final decision made, whether we are to enjoy eternal happiness or be thrown out on the rubbish-dump of the universe. From that root, egoism, self-centredness, all sin grows.

And yet the vital urge to seek what is our own good is in itself a right and natural thing. What is needed is that the mind should be enlightened and come progressively to understand that the good of the self is interwoven with the good of others, and should with justice, under the guiding-light of prudence, balance the claims of all demands, loving the neighbour as the self. Moreover, in close association with justice, there is that special virtue, the virtue of religion, which is the habit of giving God His due. The true development of the self will proceed harmoniously when justice shines beneath this loftier light, and duty to man blends in subordination with the sovereign duty to God.

It should be easy to see how prayer fits in with this preliminary scheme for the making of a good man. God made us ; He knows how we work. He takes us, to begin with, as He finds us ; He knows that the first kind of love is cupboard-love ; He knows that the moving force in us is hunger for what is good for us ; therefore He says 'Ask and you shall receive'. The prayer of petition—asking—is at the very root of prayer ; it remains an integral element, even in the sublime sacrifice of our High Priest, the Mass. It is a great force, urging us not only to ask for our daily bread, but leading us to intimate converse with Our Father, with Christ our Brother, and with their Spirit of Love, with all the angels and saints who can help us. This is the first great impulse which moves us, and if we have spoken of it as ' cupboard-love ' we have not done so contemptuously.

Now the natural result of cupboard-love, when satisfied is thankfulness. The prayer of petition opens by inevitable transition into the prayer of thanks ; and this too is part of the Mass.

But the prayer of petition has another deep purpose. It leads us equally naturally to a recognition of our dependence upon God, and this paves the way for the prayer of adoration. From the thought of the Father of lights, from whom comes every good gift and every perfect gift, we are lifted to a realisation of His power, an acknowledgement of His sovereignty, an admiration of His incomparable perfection. And all this leads toward love of His infinite goodness.

Alas, the full chord of prayer cannot be struck until another note has entered in. We are not creatures only ; we are sinners. It is only when the sombre note of sorrow and atonement blends with the rest that the chord is perfect. It is perfect in the Mass. And it is given perfect utterance in the best of all prayers, the *Our Father*. So far, then, prayer, simple, strong and deep, is revealed as the counterpart of God's design for the making of a man. It is that making, that shaping, considered from one angle, from the point of view that it is man's co-operation with God.

But this requires development. It needs to be made conscious, fully self-aware. The mind in its choices needs guidance and education. Here is the point of insertion of all that we mean by mental prayer, not exclusively in the sense of stated times spent in meditation, but embracing the full process of Christian instruction, both the presenting of doctrine to the mind and the absorption of it by the mind. And it should be evident enough that for anything like a true spiritual culture the practice of meditation is indispensable.

And the Prayer of Faith, the special subject of this book, the progressive development of a supernatural mode of knowing—how does that fit in ? More particularly, how does that gradual change in the very quality of the love that vivifies it come about ? What of the altered scale of values that begins, as was stated, with detachment from self ?

XVI

HOW THE PRAYER OF FAITH HELPS DETACHMENT

ANYONE who knows what we are talking about will recognise the fitness of an expression used by Dom Chapman in connection with it—" touches of infinity ". The characteristic mark of this prayer, as has been abundantly asserted, is an experiential awareness of the fact that God exists, usually presented to the consciousness as a ' sense ' of His presence; an awareness of the fact that He is near, not of *what* He is. But though such prayer differs from properly mystical prayer, yet between the two different phases there is continuity. It is the same supernatural life which is functioning, though it has not reached the same phase of development. And even before prayer reaches a truly or fully mystical stage, there is a dim awareness of immensity, of infinity. There are ' touches of infinity '. Now the inability to put God effectually first in our lives arises from the inability to see clearly how really ' first ' He is. In proportion as the mind grasps the truth that His is a different being from our own, that He is quite outside the series, it becomes easier to realise that there can be no comparison between Him and all else. The scale of judgments of value alters in proportion to this realisation. But the decisive alteration is made when there is a vivid apprehension of His infinitude. Now the mind can juggle with words and symbols that stand for infinity, but it cannot of its own power fill them with meaning ; we cannot grasp infinity. It is here, as well as in other ways, that the Prayer of Faith becomes powerful. The ' touches of infinity ', untranslatable though they are into the medium of the natural activities of the mind, begin to exert a decisive influence upon conduct. We begin to judge effectually that God comes first, because in that light which is darkness, in that night of faith, we have sensed the presence of an overwhelming Being, of One Who knows no bounds and no limitations. We have glimpsed, as through closed eyes, a light beyond all light. We whisper with à Kempis in awe ' O Pelagus intransnatabile '.

But this is not the beginning. The beginning is detachment from self. " If any man will come after me, let him deny himself "—that is the first step. The clog that effectively hinders our putting God first is our clinging to ourselves.

Now manifestly the training in detachment from self must start very early—cannot start too early—in life. Evidently also it is the special aim of meditation, for meditation must always be related to conduct. There is little probability of anyone making progress in prayer which will lead to the Prayer of Faith, unless by means of meditation he reaches a well-informed idea of what self-centring means and achieves in actuality a thorough conquest of it, in all its more obvious forms.

But in the life of prayer, as in other spheres, it is characteristic of God's gentleness to coax and spoil us a little at first ; he does not give meat to babes but milk. In our first discoveries of the meaning of love we find it hard to distinguish between the delight we experience in the emotions of tenderness, and the love itself ; and this is true also of the love of God which grows in prayer, notably through meditation. It requires no little acuteness of perception to distinguish what we are giving to God from what we are receiving. There is a great deal of attachment to self hidden amid the quite lawful delights we found in loving God. It is no longer sinful self-attachment, for it is no longer contrary to God's commandments ; but it is an imperfection that must be removed so that greater growth may follow. It is here that the emptying and drying which is characteristic of the Prayer of Faith begins to search out and burn away this form of self-attachment. For though the consolation we may find in affective prayer, the delight of feeling that we do love God and that He does love us, is in itself a very good thing, a thing to be prayed for and gladly enjoyed when it comes, yet attachment to self is wrong, and the symptom of this attachment would in this instance be making that consolation our aim ; it would be thinking of it as a due and proper return for our good will in loving God, so that when it ceased we felt injured, or slightly resentful, or at least gave in to the camouflaged resentment which makes us remark to ourselves some-what bitterly that we knew we did not deserve affection and are not a bit surprised that God Himself has grown tired of us.

This secret attachment to self the Holy Spirit begins to sandpaper away even in the earliest days of prayer, by the up-and-down movement of alternating consolation and desolation, which then takes the form largely of a rise and fall in the warmth of the affection we experience. But the prolonged dryness of the Prayer of Faith is even more effective in searching out the buried tap-roots of it. It might be easier to endure seasonal ups-and-downs, that we could explain by circumstances of fatigue or harassing occupation ; but when it appears to be all ' down ', when it looks as if all delight had flown for ever, then not only do we need patience of the kind that won the war for Britain—a patience ready to endure not for a stated period but indefinitely, ' until victory is achieved ' —but also we require great faith to believe that in spite of appearances God is good and loving. Here the imperceptible nourishment of the Prayer of Faith is our salvation.

For the light that it sheds on the mind gradually reveals to us that it is a much greater love to love God without any comfort, than to be lapped in tender affection. The negative process, the emptying of ideas and imagery and the flickering out of emotion, makes it possible for us to strengthen our will-love without a misleading absorption in delights that appear to be our gift to God but are really satisfaction for ourselves. The positive process, the strengthening of the supernatural element, if it be in a trough of desolation, acts upon our faith at its foundations, by causing us to renew ' acts of faith ', made in the darkness, simply by intellect and will, without any awareness of supernatural aid ; and if it be at a peak of consolation offers us a joy and a peace in the felt presence of God, which is inexpressibly more satisfying and more strengthening than the emotional delight of earlier days. Moreover if the wave mounts to a notable peak, it may flow over into the mind and the imagination and give us a vivid realisation of some truth—for instance the truth that just when God seems most to have forgotten us then He is most loving us, and is drawing from our souls a splendour of selfless love of Him. Such a vivid realisation will probably stream down into the feelings also, and fill us with affections sweeter than ever, but increasingly spiritual, seeming to vibrate not in the nervous system but in the soul itself.

The question—it may be remembered—which was the clue we began to follow in this part of the book was this : how does the dark Prayer of Faith, by influencing the shape of the mind, by acting on the knowledge-factor in prayer, come to dissolve self-attachment and liberate in the soul the tremendous force of divine charity, so that the soul can say ' I love now, not I, but the Spirit of Christ loveth in me ' ? To follow the clue, we noted first of all that self-love is radically a good and natural force in our make-up, but that it is a perilously-balanced apparatus that can easily fall over into selfishness or egoism. The work of organising a personality correctly begins with the ordinary human affair of developing altruism, the spirit of team-work, applied to all the various relations of the individual to his neighbours, and sovereignly to God. But God is not merely the highest step in a ladder or Scale of Perfection. " We shall say much and yet we shall want words, but the sum of our words is He is all."[40] There is therefore needed, to accomplish the full design God set Himself in creation, a lifting of the creature absolutely beyond its powers ; for the relation of reasonable give-and-take, of reciprocal justice, which would lead to a harmonious adjustment among creatures, is not adequate to sustain in a creature a completely satisfactory relation to God. It would be good enough to eliminate evil ; the virtue of religion, practised according to the lights and capacities of a created mind, would eliminate rebellion, blasphemy, ingratitude, indifference, and would result in dutiful recognition of God's claims to love ; but just because God, as He really is, is quite beyond the range of created intelligence, there could never be a truly adequate response on the part of the creature to the uncreated Holiness, ' laudabilis et gloriosus et superexaltatus in saecula '. Finite intelligence is necessarily unfinished in a sense ; the supernatural uplifting, though it does not belong to nature, is yet called for, appealed for, by the very helplessness of that nature, and is a fitting crown, the only fitting crown, to the work God took in hand. What we are concerned with at the moment is that this uplifting is the complete and all-purifying cure for the endemic malady of egoism, hereditary in the very blood of man since the tragedy of the Fall. It is the cure because it effects a transposition of the centre and focus of the appetite for good ; it causes the soul to seek primarily, above all, beyond all, and without any comparison to anything else, the good of God for God, in pure disinterested love of Him for His own sake, willing that He should be what He is, rejoicing that He is what He is, seeking His profit, His benefit, His success, under the name of His ' glory ', desiring that His name should be hallowed, that His kingdom should come, and that His will should be done on earth as it is in heaven. This transposition is achieved by the pouring forth into our hearts of the Holy Spirit, who is God's Love, and Who is the *Holy* Spirit precisely because He loves the uncreated infinitude of the divine nature above all else.

But the preliminary to it for us is detachment from self, because attachment to self means clinging to the old focus, keeping self as the centre. The Prayer of Faith operates on the knowledge-factor in prayer, to bring this about, by giving to the soul its first effectual ' taste ' of God. The ' touches of infinity ' arouse in us an awe-inspiring awareness of infinity, but they also lead to another realisation : that the overwhelming Being whose approach is heard like a mighty wind blowing through the stratosphere of the soul, is a Being Who deserves love, who is lovable, loveworthy, and that to a degree, to an intensity, which is not a degree at all but the edge of a shore tumbling over into unfathomable immensities. Caught on the swirl of that whirlpool the mind sees its first glimpse of what it is to love God above all things.

But the beginning is detachment from self. Suppose you were a tube of paint in an artist's paint-box : what would detachment be ? The egoist tube would rattle itself out of its groove, pushing itself into the painter's way, clamouring to be used, caring nothing for the design of the picture but only to get on to the canvas. Detachment from self would mean entering into the artist's dream of his masterpiece, desiring its fulfilment, and being content to be used, or left unused, exactly as the painter required for the perfection of his work. It is this attitude of complete and unconditional responsiveness to God's good pleasure, this utterly disinterested desire that his masterpiece should be perfected, which is detachment from self. How different from the conception of one who regards prayer as a time in which God is expected to caress the soul ! The Prayer of Faith, with its long drilling in emptiness and desolation, leads us slowly but surely to a state in which it is all one to us whether we are in sunlight or in cloud, provided only that on our part there is complete, unreserved, un-calculating, unrestricted yielding of our whole being into God's hands.

And it is this which is the never-ceasing activity which underlies even the apparently most paralytic inactivity in the desolations of this prayer. It is this factor whose presence, we suggested, could be shown by the simple process of ceasing from it. It is a grip of the will which is none the less active because it is not moving.

XVII

QUIETIST CHIMERA

YET such detachment from self is very far removed from the error of those who think that pure and perfect love of God excludes the longing to enjoy His sweetness. It is nothing so fantastic or chimerical that we are speaking of. Detachment from self is another name for the right love of self; that love is the love God wills we should have, and in the end it will be in perfect harmony with His own love, whose bountiful design it is to fill us to the brim with all delight, and above all with the delighted enjoyment of His own incomparable beauty and goodness.

There is no question of propounding here an absurdity like Quietism, or suggesting that detachment from self means an inert quiescence. One might as well say that the perfect dancing partner is the girl who is like a sack of potatoes. God is not honoured any more than we should be, by a love that prides itself on its impassivity; we do not approach to selfless love by approaching a Buddhist insensibility, nor is the delicate and eager responsiveness of a love wholly centred in God similar even remotely to the frozen pride of Quietism; it is the Quietist, not the lover of God, who can confuse an utterly self-disregarding love with that frost-bite of the soul that Quietism vaunted for holiness.

And yet what we are trying to say can only be forcibly expressed by such paradoxical statements as Our Lord's " He that will lose his life shall save it ". The detachment from self towards which the Prayer of Faith assists us is so complete, so penetrating, hunts out our hidden egoisms with a tooth-comb of such fineness, that even the elect may be deceived and be tempted to confuse it with Quietism. It may even make it look as if we did not care whether we reached the enjoyment of God, provided only that He were all in all. But this is only the paradox that inevitably enters into our utterance when the infinite has entered in. Compared to the infinite, all things are nothing. Compared to the supernaturalised will to set God and God alone sovereignly above all things, even our own hunger for Him is dwarfed to nothingness, like a marble measured against the Cosmos. But for all that it is a very precious little marble to us ; it is our all, as far as our own satisfaction is concerned ; and to the tender all-seeing eyes of God it is a jewel He will shatter the rocks to win.

It is, after all, only rarely that there is need to warn folk against mistaking suicide of the heart for love of God, as they did at Port-Royal. The hearts of common folk are much too alive and kicking for that ; they are squirming, palpitating, bleeding. Only perhaps in a withered intellectualism like that of the eighteenth century does that weed thrive. Our Lord crowded it out of His harvest-field by the lavish sowings of the revelations of His Sacred Heart. He cried in anguish that He wanted us to feel ; the " indifference " He was seeking is an exquisite, delicate sensibility, so supercharged with responsive love for the divine Goodness as to judge that in comparison with that Goodness all things else are nothing ; but we shall not come to such great love except through tender sympathy and human affection for his suffering human Heart. He wants us to want Him.

No; it is not towards a marble acquiescence that the Prayer of Faith will lead us. Nevertheless it will lead us through such icy ravines and across such blistering glaciers that we shall often wonder whether our souls have not been chilled to marble. Let us try to understand. The process that is in course of evolution in our life of prayer is the process of transformation by which the grub of humanity is becoming the butterfly of grace. The vital spark of divine charity has been lodged in the soul; it is destined to glow and spread and finally break out into the dancing flames of perfect charity in heaven. Now two things go to the making of love: knowledge and the grasp of the will. In these pages we have attempted to outline first how the process of transformation ordinarily affects the soul's knowledge in this life; now we are considering more especially the grasp of the will. In the sphere of knowledge there is a progressive development of the power of faith, which results in a diminution of natural activity, as a temporary consequence of readjustment; there is an in-between stage of almost total darkness, like the moment of streaming eyes when a brilliant light suddenly floods a room at night. Now we are saying that similarly there is a change, and an intervening period of emptiness apparently, in the grasp of will. Only it is not so noticeable; at least not so soon noticeable; the perceptible, unmistakable " change of gear " belongs usually to a later development in prayer than the Prayer of Faith with which we are in the main concerned. The emergence of the new state of things will be heralded by some ' night of the spirit ', some purifying pain more intense than has been previously experienced.

The real transformation that is taking place in our souls, whether we are aware of it or not, is the energising of our wills by divine charity. The " change of gear " is our conscious perception of the change wrought in our wills by grace. The intervening period—the long stretch of icy ravines and blistering glaciers—is the period in which all the natural warmth of our human wills is temporarily removed in order that deep down the fire of charity may smoulder and spread through our wills. But the " change of gear " is usually later because of a special value of love arising from faith. If we pause here to examine this, it will give us heart to continue more courageously through these glaciers, when in addition to our prayer being void of all that we can call activity of thought, there is also the additional trial that we seem to all intents and purposes to be devoid of any love for God.

Ordinarily speaking love is proportionate to knowledge. It is not humanly speaking possible to have actual love for a heathen Chinee of whom we have never heard. "Auld acquaintance " is the common basis of friendly affection. And the reason why this is so is that love is a response on our part to lovableness in another ; its first demand is that the other should somehow, in our eyes, be worthy of being loved, should deserve it, should kindle in us a glow of delight which is spontaneous. Yet at the same time it is essential to the love of true friendship that it should be free. It is not a thing that can be bought or ordered ; the spontaneity with which it springs up in our hearts must be matched by a glad acceptance and a consciousness that if it is a gift bestowed on us—in the sense that we cannot stimulate it when it does not come of itself—yet it is at the same time a gift bestowed by us, for it is not paid as a due but is offered with all the noble liberality of freedom. It is this special value of noble freedom that God is eager to find in our love of Him. Now God is God ; He is the overwhelming all-lovableness whose entrancing beauty whirls into the vortex of unutterable joy every living thing that beholds the splendour of His Being ; if we saw Him as He is, we should not be free ; we should be swept helplessly along the torrent of His delights unable to do anything but yield ourselves to the irresistible attractiveness of the infinite Good.

Therefore His wisdom has found a way by which we can truly reach Him, can give our love to Him directly, and yet retain the unfettered liberality of friendship. He has found the way of Faith.

By Faith (which is called a theological virtue because it relates directly to God) we reach God Himself; yet such is the character of the knowledge born of faith that seeing we see not, we know the one living God, yet remain unconstrained by His unbearable beauty, free to present before Him the priceless offering of friendship. By the way of faith He has hidden yet revealed Himself, and He has done this, not exclusively because He desired to be well-pleased in our gift of friendship, but also because He wished us to deserve, as far as any created insignificance could deserve it, His own most royal return of friendship; He wished to have this reason for loving us, so that His munificence might have yet another channel through which to pour the prodigal torrent of His delights.

And this is the mysterious worth of faith, that it is a knowledge which abrogates the common law that love is proportionate to knowledge. It enables us to give to God a love out of all proportion to the feeble conceptions of Him that illustrate our human minds. For it is a knowledge that is an ' unknowing ', and it is the starting-point of a love that is nothing less than divine charity itself.

Therefore is it that since that divine charity is already in operation, making our lives worthy of even the Infinite Majesty's pleasure in them, yet He withholds from us for a long time a full awareness of what love we are giving Him; because by this means He can bring forth in us the special treasures of unconstrained loyalty, a loyalty that endures even against appearances, and of free and liberally-given friendship.

XVIII

PURIFYINGS AND PASSIVITIES

So the Prayer of Faith aids us to detachment from self,
both by weaning us from the pleasures our human powers
found at first in prayer, and by giving us a first dim
inkling of the infinity of God. It also fans the flame
of supernatural love, feeding it on the mysterious blind
knowledge that is faith. Hence the general trend of
development we are likely to notice in prayer, in the
sphere of knowledge, is a lessening of natural activity,
accompanied by an increasing awareness of God. Along
with this change, there is a parallel change in the sphere
of love. This, as we said, is less easy to observe or
analyse. But the total impression of the change is
instinctively expressed by the use of some word like
" quiet ". Our will (that is, our love) seems like a top,
spinning so steadily that it no longer quivers or sways ;
in fact it appears motionless. When in addition to this
poise or unthrobbing spin of the will there is also a
peaceful contentment in the sphere of knowledge, a
satisfied resting in the blind clasp of God by supernatural
awareness, some such name as Quietude or Prayer of
Quiet will seem appropriate. The manifold variations
due to relative restlessness in the natural faculties, which
may alter the impression of quiet, have given rise to
a variety of names for the various states. The chief
objection to these names is that they provoke an unprofitable curiosity, all the more unprofitable since there
is no fixed sequence in which the phenomena occur.
The impression of quiet, when arising especially from
stillness in the sphere of knowledge, leads to such

characteristic language as St. Teresa employs in stating that the will alone is employed.[41] This is evidently a *façon de parler*, but the point is not of much practical importance, and discussion of it might lead into scholastic subtleties concerning the distinctness of the faculties of knowing and loving which would be out of place in these pages.

Now, broadly speaking, the further trend of prayer on the side of knowledge is towards the emergence of a supernatural realisation of *what* God is. This, we suggested, is what might be called specifically mystical prayer, and as such is beyond the scope of this book. At the same time, we hinted, there is a corresponding trend towards a change in the state of will, or the quality of the love that is experienced. We have described it briefly as the beginning of the awareness of supernatural love that is energising in our wills. Alternatively—or complementarily, that is, looking at the same thing from the other side—it would be an experiential sense of tremendous attraction of us by God. This, clearly, is the counterpart of the supernatural realisation of what He is. (At such a point as this it becomes more than ever difficult to speak or think of knowing and loving in separation from each other.) When this is very intense, and more especially when the human organism is less adjusted to the new type of experience, it will tend to lead to a series of phenomena—decreasing as the adjustment grows—to which belong rapture and ecstasy. These also, since they belong to specifically mystical prayer, are out of our present scope. All that we wish to add about the trend towards the " change of gear " —that is towards an experiential awareness of the supernatural element in our love—is to amplify a comment made earlier, namely that this trend is heralded by what St. John of the Cross calls the Night of the Spirit, the second part of the Dark Night of the Soul. The practical point of the remark is simply this : if the unbearable aridity of the Prayer of Faith turns into a realistic rendering of hell within your soul, do not be alarmed. The theoretical part of the remark is this : the essence of the " Night of the Spirit " is a purifying of the *will*, a tearing away from the soul of the last tendrils of egoism ; the means employed may vary enormously, and may include non-supernatural elements like bodily suffering, but the characteristic means operate through the supernatural abilities of which the soul has acquired the use, notably an experience beyond the range of reason of some truth that burns the soul, such as the meaning of sin, the appalling holiness of God, the mystery of the unfathomable nothingness of created being. Not only do these means vary very much in kind, but, I would suggest they vary also in the equation *intensity* $\times$ *duration* ; they will tend to be brief but beyond endurance, or more tolerable but proportionately prolonged.[42] The latter appears to be more typical of our age. But the motive for alluding here to the " Night of the Spirit " was simply the double one of reassuring those who are frightened by some inexplicable horror that seems to be invading their souls ; and to caution those who are apt to mistake a little sensible consolation coming in the midst of prolonged aridity for the mystical espousals of the Bride and the Lamb ; if such a transport of delight has not been preceded by spiritual sufferings that defy all attempt to describe them, it is better to assume that the transport is a ray of early spring sunlight. The Night of the Spirit is a fully mounted offensive directed against attachment to self. It is there that the effectiveness of it should be studied, and if it is asked how we can enter into the mansions of which it is the door, Our Lord has given the answer : " If any man will come after Me, let him deny himself."

We may take occasion at this point to touch on another matter that sometimes gives rise to queries or anxieties, though it is somewhat beyond the scope of a book dealing with the Prayer of Faith. It is the question of ' passivity ' in prayer. Properly speaking the question arises, or should arise, as a matter of experience. It ought not to trouble anyone, except when it happens. But in practice it is more likely to cause difficulty as a matter of secondhand experience, as something read about in other people's experience. It is liable to enter the field of vision under two aspects : first of all, in reading the spiritual journals of souls of prayer one encounters numerous descriptions of the soul being carried away as by a force from outside itself, prayer becoming a passive acceptance rather than an active employment; secondly, in reading books about prayer, one becomes aware of discussion and divided opinion, the dominant trend of which is emphasis on the existence of certain 'infused' forms of prayer, sharply distinguished from the 'acquired' forms. The division of opinion is mainly as to what is acquired and what is infused, and whether or not there is an 'acquired contemplation'. The solid agreement of opinion is on the point that mystical prayer, properly so-called, does not lie within volitional control, but is an entirely free gift of God; all we can do is to prepare the way for it.

The preoccupation of writers who insist strongly on the point that mystical prayer is 'infused' is apparently to prevent silly people thinking they are mystics when they are nothing of the sort. The impression given is that the writers lived at a time when it was much in fashion to flatter oneself that one was soaring in the empyrean of the mystic life.

The trouble is that for those who really know what is being talked about the warning is unnecessary, while for those who do not the recognition-test is capable of being misapplied. The danger that has to be guarded against, in this matter of passivity in prayer (apart from that of fancying oneself 'advanced') is the danger of mistaking idleness for passivity; and the other side of this knife-edge danger is mistaking passivity for idleness. You may go wrong because you think you are being 'carried' in prayer, when the fact is that you are comfortably curled up in a hollow in the hillside, dreaming that you are skipping on the crest; but you may equally go wrong by straining to achieve natural activity at a time when your soul is really though imperceptibly occupied in a supernatural activity. How is one to tell?

In practice, by leaving the question of ' passivity ' to the experts. It is no use trying to judge whether one is duly active, or has been rendered passive, by the feel of it. There are days when throwing pancakes seems to be done by a preternatural assistance from one's guardian angel, so amazingly easy does it seem. There are other days when it is difficult to avoid getting the wrong foot into the wrong slipper, so much does everything go wrong. A similar phenomenon of alternating ease and travail in the realm of prayer might confuse a person who was unhealthily interested in ' passive states in prayer '. The practical attitude is a balancing of two forces, like the two sets of muscles which are used for instance in making a groove in a piece of wood with a gouge; one set applies force in the direction required; the other is ready to check the tool the moment it slips or goes wrong. So in this matter of passivity in prayer we ought to be yielding to every impulse of grace, yet ready to counter our own tendency to do nothing, the moment we realise that we literally are doing nothing. When, in one way or another, we are being ' carried ' by a facility in praying, whether it be simply an ease in meditating, or such a surge of spiritual intensity as lifts us to a love of God that we cannot believe is our own doing, we should correspond as well as we can. When on the contrary everything seems dead, we should sustain a quiet pressure of the will, bearing on whatever activity is possible to us, whether it be discursive meditation or merely a dogged determination not to stop prayer before the appointed time. Such an attitude will at once preclude the danger of laziness and prevent the other danger of our hindering grace by clinging too much to our familiar ways. But this note is really for those who have not experienced a real passivity in prayer, and are only wondering if they have ; when they do, they will not be asking questions like that any more.

It is of little practical help to know in what degree our prayer at any given moment is ' passive ' in a technical sense. That in any case is a knowledge that is doubly masked, first by the unpredictable alternation of ease and travail in prayer which engages the natural faculties, and secondly because even in prayer that is supernatural the first experience is likely to appear to us as ' given ' or ' infused ' whereas when that state has grown habitual it will be likely to appear to us more as our own, though not necessarily as something we can achieve at will —but, for the matter of that, as we have already noted, the same thing may be felt about quite natural activities ; for instance the ability to write poetry is a natural ability that nevertheless appears to come by ' inspiration ' from outside, and not to be under complete volitional control. The double masking therefore renders difficult what is in any event otiose, namely a self-conscious effort to estimate one's position on the *Scala Perfectionis*.

These last remarks are really intended for persons who because they are enjoying an unaccustomed facility in prayer—more especially if their state is one of vivid awareness of God accompanied by ideas and emotions that seem to have the character of ' lights '—begin to wonder if they have reached what they had read about, a passive state in prayer. The gist of the advice is : do not think about it. Passivity in prayer, like chastity, is the better attained the less we advert to it. As regards such experiences in prayer as are genuinely passive in the technical sense, they belong to the time when the path is running along the crest of the ridge, and those who have them will not require advice of this kind. They are more likely to require assurance that they are not deluded, because their humility being greater they will be less inclined to trust their own judgments, and

for such assurance they will need to be under obedience
to a director.

XIX

THE PRAYER OF FAITH
AND SORROW FOR SIN

BRIEFLY to review once more our line of thought, it is
this. All Christian prayer derives its worth from faith
vitalised by charity. ' My just man lives by faith '
is true more in this sphere than anywhere. Faith is a
supernatural elevation of our natural power of knowing
by accepting truth from others. This elevation of the
power does not eliminate the natural power which it
transforms. The beginning of prayer is therefore a
raising of the mind and heart to God, which, as perceived
in the consciousness of the person praying, is just like
any normal human thinking and loving. But there is
from the beginning a supernatural element present in
this seemingly natural activity, and the usual history of
a soul's prayer is the gradual emergence of this element
into the field of consciousness. For a period it centres
in the strengthening of an awareness of God as a reality,
often felt as present in the soul, but not ' seen '; that
is there is no knowledge of what God is, other than
what has been acquired through the common channel
of revelation. According to individual patterns as
numerous and varied as the persons who are praying,
this developing awareness of God's reality is accompanied
by a general trend towards simplification or synthesis in
the intellect's grasp of revelation, and then by a certain
fluctuating paralysis or muffling of this activity. The
purpose of this is to concentrate the focus of attention
on the awareness of God's reality or presence. The
fluctuation may have as a counterpart an increasing
clarity in the intellect's grasp of revelation, a more vivid

acceptance of the Faith, which is actually more a matter of will and readiness to believe, than an articulate increase in the sum of knowledge. This is more likely to be observed in ' spiritual reading ' outside the time of prayer. It is the flowering of the Holy Spirit's Gift of Understanding, one of the blooms of the maturing plant which is the virtue of faith.

Along with the trend towards synthesis or unification in the sphere of knowledge there is likely to be a steadying and intensifying of emotion, like the stillness of a spinning top. Along with the muffling or paralysis that usually follows, there is likely to be a deepening perception of the meaning of detachment from self and a more vigorous resistance to egoism. It is in proportion as the all-transcending majesty of the divine Goodness is discerned that the clinging of disordered self-love is snapped. And this, more than anything else, is the objective and aim of prayer, during this often much-prolonged phase which we have named the Prayer of Faith.

Now there is one strand, indispensably woven into the texture of all prayer, about which we have said little. It is one of the most vitally important. It is sorrow for sin. Let us try now to see the bearing of the Prayer of Faith upon our sorrow.

Faith, as we understand it in the beginning of life, is like a brown-paper parcel, which we know contains something of immeasurable value, but which we have not yet opened. The Prayer of Faith is a peeping into the parcel, through chinks in the wrapping. Among the dazzling jewels we dimly become aware of three which have a special concern with our sorrow for our sins ; they are truths which because of a factor of infinity in them are not fully comprehensible to the grasp of reason, and it is by making us inexpressibly aware of infinitude that the Prayer of Faith makes them dynamic forces energising in our sorrow.

One is the holiness of God. " Hallowed be Thy name," we pray, but apart from the fact that it takes us long to realise the richness of the Hebrew expression 'Thy name', and to relate it to the very Being of the all-holy God, we are also hampered by having a very threadbare idea of what holiness is. We tend to associate it with those whom we regard as holy persons, and to identify it with blamelessness of conduct. A flash of grandeur from some holy place, the impressive splendour of some majestic ritual in an imposing cathedral, may reveal to us that holiness is the indwelling of God.

Memories of the Holy of Holies in the Temple under the Old Law, the reverence we accord to the consecrated chalices of the Mass, or moments of awe when at the " Sanctus, Sanctus, Sanctus, Dominus Deus sabaoth " our faith discerns myriads of angels prostrate before the mysterious heights of the Divinity—these things may begin to form in our minds a faint impression of God's holiness. We shall look with a new reverence, almost fear, upon persons who we have been told are holy persons, and shall respect more deeply the sacramental consecration that is upon bishops and priests. But the thing itself outshines our eyes. The holiness of God is ineffable. It is that by reason of which He is exalted, infinitely and inaccessibly, beyond all being save His own; it is that majesty of illimitable power, that resplendent glory of flawless and uncircumscribed perfection, that inexhaustible ocean of indefectible love, that incomprehensible simplicity of being whose essence is existence—it is God. And sin is an insufferable flouting of the majesty of God.

The second of these jewels is the creative love of God. To grasp it at all we have to gaze with bewildered eyes into the unfathomable abyss of non-existence. It is virtually impossible for us to do so. Our experience starts from self-awareness. The one constant factor underlying it all is ourself. To conceive of that very self as a film of bubble-surface on which the patterns come and go, and beneath which there is nothingness, is frightening; we do not do it. But the realisation that beneath it there is not nothing, but the creative love of God, is an experience that transmutes all reality for us. Sin is a repulsing of that infinite gentleness, of that sustaining hand at once so strong and so deft that we rest wholly upon it and do not know that it is touching us at all.

The third jewel is the counterpart of the second. It is the astonished vision of the nothingness of created existence, in proportion to the reality of God. It is that which lends anger, righteous anger against ourselves, to the terror and regret that begin to be the dynamic forces in our sorrow for sin.

Emotional sorrow is good. We ought to feel sorrow if we can, and to pray earnestly for a *felt* contrition, using those considerations which the catechism tells us will lead to sorrow for our sins. And the time of prayer of which meditation is the characteristic activity, a time especially consonant with a retreat, is the time for labouring to secure this sorrow. Hence the Ignatian Exercises do not ignore the steps that will lead to this end. But just as the satisfactions of affective prayer are apt to mask from us the shortcomings of our spiritual life, and to absorb our energies rather than to canalise them for action, so the intensity of felt contrition has an inherent weakness; it is liable to prove something of a satisfaction to ourselves, and to leave us, in the reaction that follows it, less vigilantly vigorous in attacking our egoism. So it tends to disappear with growth in prayer, being replaced by an aversion from sin which is even more powerful in its effect on conduct. This is the special effect of the Prayer of Faith, opening the eyes of the soul as it does to the infinities that underlie the fact of sin, revealing as it does the first glimpse of these jewels.

XX

THE PRAYER OF FAITH
AND THE PASSION

ONE of the considerations leading to sorrow for sin is that by our sins we have crucified again to ourselves the Son of God, making Him a mockery. And one of the most potent of the graces that can be bestowed upon us by Our Lord is the favour of being drawn to contemplate in prayer His sufferings. It is especially in reference to the Passion that the rule holds good— we ought to continue making use of the help the imagination and the emotions may give as long as they are a help, and we should not be misled by any wrong notions of the value of the Prayer of Faith into repressing such assistance to our sanctification. Even St. John of the Cross, as noted above, excepts the Sacred Humanity from his exhortations to souls to give up as soon as possible the use of the lower faculties in prayer. But when, whatever we may wish, the ability to use the imagination ceases, we must not think that the consideration just mentioned will lose its force. Quite the contrary. The Venerable Marie de l'Incarnation writes : " In this state of prayer which had deprived it of the support which it was receiving from the Sacred Humanity of Our Lord, my soul saw clearly and by a vivid realisation that it had gained much, and that this privation, though at first sharp and surprising, had been only to make it go forward in the good favours of His divine Majesty."[43]

What the Prayer of Faith does especially is this : even in the tenderest sorrow for the Passion of Christ as the outcome of our sins, there is apt to be at first an alloy

of self-love ; the regret that by our sins we have disgraced
ourselves may give place to the nobler sorrow that by
them we have cost Him suffering, but we cannot at first
exclude a tinge of bitterness on this account ; now
bitterness is one of the surest symptoms of lurking
egoism ; the Prayer of Faith, by revealing the allness
of God, shows also the splendour of His redemption
of us ; by transposing the focus of our love it makes
us see the Passion from Our Lord's point of view ; the
tinge of regret which is self-centred gives place to a joy
that He was able to manifest His adorable goodness even
by His Passion ; we begin to understand St. Paul's
words : " I will glory in my weakness, so that the power
of Christ is displayed through me " ; and we understand
the joy of the angels upon one sinner doing penance,
and the mysterious ' O felix culpa ' of the Church's
Easter liturgy. This comes from that profound effect
of the Prayer of Faith which makes our love truly centre
in God, loving self only as belonging to Him.

XXI

DETACHMENT FROM ONE'S OWN HOLINESS

ANOTHER result is concerned not so much with sin as
with an even subtler form of self-attachment. This is
attachment to our own holiness. Now it would be absurd
and wrong not to desire holiness. This would be simply
another form of the absurdity of thinking that we should
love God better if we had no longing to enjoy His beauty
and His love. Nevertheless, here too there is need of
the paradox " He that will lose his life shall save it ".
There is just the difference between desiring to be holy
for our own benefit, and desiring it for God's sake.
The Prayer of Faith, by its transmuting of our love,
leads us to desire holiness with an ardent desire, which

does not eliminate but simply ignores what in itself is a good thing, namely seeking holiness as an advantage to ourselves; but which makes paramount the motive of seeking it for God's sake, in order to be ' in laudem gloriae ejus ' (unto the praise of His glory)[44] and in order to delight the Heart of Christ. This change checks the discontent and bitterness with which we are inclined to view our own disappointing lack of progress after so many years of striving. From it there springs that longanimity, that perfected patience, which finds even in our own involuntary unsatisfactoriness the life-giving Cross. It dispels the secret envies and jealousies which mar even lovely souls. For if the one thing that matters to us is the design of God, it will not matter at all whether we are a high-light in His painting or just a small brown patch in a corner, unnoticed by any eyes but His.

XXII

HUMILITY

FAITH is a form of worship. It is in the first place the tribute we pay to the all-truthfulness of God, by accepting what He tells us, even though it appears to run counter to the assurances of our senses and the inclinations of our reason. The Prayer of Faith begins with that humble adoration. It leads on to a humility which is a joy to God. For humility only begins as a kind of seeing; it becomes a kind of loving. The humble worship of an act of faith unseals our eyes, wiping from them the stickiness of pride. Then we begin to see the truth, and the first step in humility is to see the truth about ourselves. This dispels the crooked illusions, that come from vanity and conceit. But that is only the beginning. For humility to be a kind of loving, it has to become a rejoicing in the truth about ourselves.

Now it is this joy which springs from the Prayer of Faith.

It springs in this way. The light that this prayer brings to the soul is above all light about God. Though in it we do not see what God is in Himself, yet we begin to be aware of His infinity. We begin to realise the truth that God is, and that in comparison with Him we are not. Our shadow of being is nearer to nothing than it is to His fullness. Now God knows this. He is the Truth and He loves truth. If we recognise and acknowledge that Divine Being is the one sovereign treasure and created being is only shadow, we are joining with Him in making truth shine forth, and He loves that and is pleased. It is not that God is jealous and grasping and resents others trying to scramble on to His throne; actually He is so generous that what He wants to do is to make us sit with Him on the throne, to be ' *participes ejus divinitatis* ', sharers in His godhead. But there must be truth. He cannot allow our climbing to the throne to be based on falsehood, on the absurd assertion that of ourselves " we are gods " and have a right to climb. That is the pride that has perverted Satan and his angels. God loves humility because humility is truth. The Prayer of Faith, by bringing to our souls the splendid realisation that God is God and there is nothing like to Him, illumines them with the lovely radiance of this humility.

But to be perfect humility must become a way of loving. What prevents this is attachment to self. The rooted impulse to achieve selfhood, to develop oneself, to become someone, is in itself a good thing. But when it is allowed to make itself the focus of our existence it becomes bad, it becomes egoism. The way to overcome this badness is love, love of God as the absolutely sovereign treasure, love of God which makes us glad with a selfless gladness that God is God, that He is in His own right and by His own self-existent being the one all-deserving, love-worthy Goodness. " One is good,

God." It is when we begin to be glad of this that we begin to understand humility, for the correlative movement of the heart is joy that in comparison with God we are nothing. This is an utterly selfless joy. It is inconceivable except as a delight springing from love that really has God for its centre. And it is the full flowering of humility.

It is not that on our own account it pleases us to know how insignificant we are; it would be a perversion to love nothingness for its own sake; it is simply that on God's account we rejoice in His greatness, and the vision of the abysmal nothingness of created existence becomes simply a lake-surface, looking upon which we see mirrored the super-exalted magnificence of Him Who Is. Humility becomes love because it is a glad acceptance of the truth that we are wholly His.

The Prayer of Faith brings about this transmutation of our wills, not only because it brings that imperceptible light which gradually evokes in our souls a dim awareness of divinity, but also because its long desolations and interminable dryness, if rightly accepted, bring about a penetrating detachment from self which is the prelude to such love.

The soul exulting in the grandeurs and the infinite lovableness of God not only rejoices in the truth of its dependence upon creative love, but so rejoices that if it were possible that it should be offered a choice between being His, on the one hand, and existing independently of Him, on the other, it would have no hesitation: existence not in loving subordination to Him would be a mockery; better the blankness of utter annihilation than a state of existence—if such a thing were conceivable—that did not draw all its sweetness from Him Who is the source of all good.

More than this: in a folly of love, knowing well that nothing can be added to the infinite, the soul would yet wish, were it not an absurdity, to surrender even its little drop of being if by so doing it could add to the glory and greatness of Him who is worthy of all love. And although this is a fond fancy of love, it is not utterly removed from reality. For while it is true that nothing can be added to the Infinite, yet mysteriously something can. God creates a universe without undergoing any change in Himself; that is a mystery beyond our grasp. The love of the human Heart of Christ does not increase the everlasting love with which God loves us, and yet it is real. So, too, though we can add nothing to the splendours of divine Being and can make no increase in the ocean of His felicity, yet our acceptance of Him as God is real. By that humility with which we lovingly acknowledge His sovereignty we crown Him God of the little kingdom of ourselves, we give Him this glory and it is something real, though it is external to His divinity. And the profounder our perception of our nothingness before Him, the wider is the kingdom we open to Him. If that perception is lit with love, and joy in our dependence, then we are offering Him a throne in our soul which His Majesty will not disdain. Such is the humility which springs from the Prayer of Faith.

XXIII

SUMMING UP

SUCH then, to sum up, is what we have meant by the " Prayer of Faith " : a light, lit in the depths of the soul at the moment of baptism, brightening the powers of the mind so that even from infancy the teachings of God through His Church are accepted and become the knowledge by which love is lifted to God ; brightening those powers to translucency until more and more clearly the image and reflection of God is perceived in His creation ; brightening them to transparency until it is more than an image, it is the very stir and movement of God which is perceived in that creation; finally shining out through the natural powers in an awareness, immediate and experiential, though indefinable, of the presence of God in the soul. A fire, kindled in the will at the moment of baptism, smouldering and glowing and spreading till it breaks out into consciousness and the soul begins to be aware that the love by which it loves is the very charity of God, the Spirit who is the eternal Love of the Father and of the Son.

The Prayer of Faith is supernatural, yet it is grafted, like all the marvels of grace, on to the nature which it uplifts and transforms. There is no break seen, no visible soldering in the divine craftsmanship, yet it is the characteristic of this prayer, when regarded as a state or phase in the development of a soul, that it gradually subdues, and for a time appears to paralyse, the activities which are familiar and natural to us. Hence it is called a night.

But it is a night of ' sense ', and its positive element is another kind of day, a day which is itself subject to waxing and waning, to consolation and desolation.

It is a night, and it is a slow but potent purification whose aim is to secure complete detachment from self, as the necessary prelude to that love of God which knows no restrictions and no reserves.

We have sketched the characteristic evolution of such prayer more especially as it develops out of methodic mental prayer, from meditation and the deliberate use of imaginative thinking. But we have been at pains to emphasise that it is not only from such systematic training of the mind that this deep prayer comes. It grows no less out of a prayer that is more vocal than meditative. Christian prayer is the energising of one and the same life, the life of Him Who is the Vine, Whose branches we are, whatever may be the special way in which a soul has been moulded by circumstances. It is this unity, this leading of all roads to the same home, which we have been anxious to stress. Prayer, the raising up of the mind and heart to God, understood as a raising which means a supernaturalising, is not the privilege of the learned and the highly-trained. It can be reached by the faithful recitation of uncounted rosaries, no less than by skilful use of methods of mental prayer. It cannot be reached by anyone, however skilled and erudite, whose heart is clogged by attachment to self. It will not be reached by any save those who, striving after this detachment, are prepared to face the desolation of prayer, be it a long interminable trudging along dry sands, or a briefer ordeal of passing through the valley of the shadow of death. It may lead us, even on this side of the grave, to where the path runs along the mountain ridge, and the soul is delighted with glimpses of the beauty of God, and carried out of itself by rapturous experience of the love God has set burning within it. Or it may not lead us there. The purpose of this book was not to speak of the heights, but only to bring comfort to those who tread the sloping hills. May the divine Goodness, which alone can touch dead words and make them springs of comfort, so touch these words that they may help here and there one who walks the way of the Prayer of Faith.

NOTES

[1] Page 28. I Corinthians chap. xii, v. 3.

[2] Page 29. Cf. Philippians chap. ii, v. 5.

[3] Page 30. Cf. e.g. *The Mystical Doctrine of St. John of the Cross*, p. 100 " The third sign we have for ascertaining whether this dryness be the purgation of sense is inability to meditate and make reflections ". (Abridgement by C. H. Sheed and Ward, 1944.)

[4] Page 34. Cf. Poulain : chap. ii, n. 66 *bis*. (See note 9 for bibliog. ref.)

[5] Page 38. *Spiritual Exercises :* Rules for the Discernment of Spirits ; Rule Three.

[6] Page 45. L. de Grandmaison, S.J. *Ecrits Spirituels* (Gabriel Beauchesne, Rue de Rennes 117. Paris. 1934). Cf. tome I, p. 145.

[7] Page 51. Cf. St. Thomas Summa 2a 2ae q. 8 art. 1 Indiget ergo homo supernaturali lumine ut ulterius penetret ad cognoscendum quaedam quae per lumen naturele cognoscere non valet, et illud lumen supernaturale homini datum vocatur donum intellectus.

[8] Page 52. Cf. Luke xii, v. 42 " allowance of food at the appointed time ".

[9] Page 52. Père Brou in *S. Ignace Maître d'Oraison* cites from Guigues de Chartreux : Reading without meditation is dry ; meditation without reading goes astray. Prayer without meditation is lukewarm ; meditation without prayer is sterile. Prayer with devout contemplation imbibes nourishment ; but to reach contemplation without prayers is a rare and miraculous thing. (Scala Claustralium. Migne P.L. 184.) (*S. Ignace Maître d'Oraison*. Alex. Brou, S.J. Edition Spes. 17 Rue Soufflot, Paris.)

[10] Page 53. Passages are too numerous to cite, but for example (in the Abridgement named above) p. 30 "All these imaginations and apprehensions are to be emptied out of the soul, which must remain in darkness as far as it concerns the senses, in order that we may attain to the divine union, because they bear no proportion to the proximate means of union with God ; as neither do bodily things, the objects of the five exterior senses."

[11] Page 53. " I am treating here of a solid and substantial doctrine suited to all, if they seek to advance to that detachment

of spirit which is here described. My principal object, however, is not to address myself to all, but only to certain persons of our holy order of Mount Carmel. . . ." (Abridgement ut sup., p. 8.)

"Keep in mind, however, that I am now specially speaking of those who have begun to enter into the state of contemplation. For, as to beginners, this must be discussed at greater length, which I shall do when I shall have to treat of what is peculiar to them." (Do., p. 24.)

"Though such considerations, forms, and methods of meditation may be necessary for beginners, in order to inflame and fill their souls with love, through the instrumentality of sense, as I shall explain hereafter. . . ." (Do., p. 31.)

[12] Page 55. Cf. A. Poulain, S.J. *Les Graces d'Oraison*, chap. vi. (English translation, *The Graces of Interior Prayer*, by Leonora Yorke Smith. Kegan Paul, Trench, Trubner & Co., 1928.)

[13] Page 55. *Idem.* Chapter v.

[14] Page 61. *The Art of Contemplation*, by Ramon Lull, edited by E. Allison Peers (S.P.C.K.).

[15] Page 61. *Exercises.* First Week, Addition 3.

[16] Page 62. Cf. De Guibert, *Theologia Spiritualis*, n. 102.

[17] Page 67. Matthew vi : ' Moreover when you are at prayer, do not use many phrases, like the heathens, who think to make themselves heard by their eloquence'. (Trans. Mgr. R. A. Knox.)

[18] Page 69. Encyclical Letter of Pope Pius XII *Mystici Corporis Christi*, n. 88 (English translation, *The Mystical Body of Jesus Christ*. C.T.S., London, 1944).

[19] Page 70. Breviary, Feast of the Most Holy Rosary, October 7th. Second Nocturn.

[20] Page 73. Cf. J. Marechal, S.J., *Etudes sur la Psychologie des Mystiques*, for a discussion of this function of vocal prayer as disposing the soul for higher forms of prayer, p. 194 (Museum Lessianum. Felix Alcan, 108 Boulevard S. Germain, Paris 6. Tome I, 1924).
Cf. also *Within that City*, by Arnold Lunn, chap. xiv.

[21] Page 73. *Ecrits Spirituels*, ut sup. I, p. 167.

[22] Page 73. Cf. St. Ignatius : *Exercises*. Note on First Method of Prayer in *Tres Modi Orandi*.

[23] Page 77. *Exercises. Secunda Hebdomada : Quinta (Contemplatio).*

[24] Page 79. The name Prayer of Faith as signifying arid contemplation is by no means new. Ludovic de Besse (*The Science of Prayer*, chap. 10) enumerates various names given to this phase of prayer, this being his own preference. (*The*

Science of Prayer, by Ludovic de Besse, O.S.F.C. B. O. & W., 1925.)

[25] Page 80. Summa Theologica 2a 2ae Q LXXXIII art. 12. Translation by the English Dominican Province. B. O. & W., 1922.

[26] Page 80. Among many references that might be made on this question see Book I, chap. i, par. 2 of *Les Voies de l'Oraison Mentale*, by Vital Lehodey (Librairé Vict. Lecoffre, 90 Rue Bonaparte, Paris. English translation by a monk of Mount Melleray. Gill, 50 Upper O'Connell Street, Dublin, 1938).

[27] Page 81. This recommendation is but a much milder repetition of the vigorous counsels of St. John of the Cross.

[28] Page 84. Poulain, Op. cit. Chapter vii.

[29] Page 89. *Spiritual Letters*.

[30] Page 89. Along with ideas that thus rise spontaneously in the mind there will evidently be an emotional accompaniment; so the state of mind as a whole can be called an 'affection'. Apart from speculation whether the ideas come out of our own head or from God, there is another doubt: ought we to foster or to restrain such affections? Exception made for those of whom St. John of the Cross is speaking when he says 'Hence it becomes more evident that the fitting disposition for this union is, not that the soul should understand, taste, feel, or imagine anything on the subject of the nature of God, or any other thing whatever, but only that pureness and love which is perfect resignation, and complete detachment from all things for God alone', we may cite as encouraging such 'acts' or 'affections':—

St. Francis de Sales: *Introduction à la Vie Dévote* Pt. II, chap. vii 'C'est une règle générale qu'il ne faut jamais retenir les affections'.

Lehodey: Op. cit. Pt. 3, chap. vi, art. 5: 'Si au contraire notre âme est inclinée a faire des actes tranquilles ou ardents, et si les affections jaillissent comme de source, laissons-nous aller sans contrainte à cet attrait; une telle occupation ne saurait être que très profitable dès lors que c'est la grace qui la provoque.'

Pt. 2, chap. ix, art. 6: 'Il y a les mêmes motifs . . . pour ne pas supprimer de parti pris les affections que l'on peut facilement faire'.

[31] Page 89. *Interior Castle* Sixth Mansion, chap. vii, par. 8. Reference to Ascent of Mount Carmel, 3-1-12.

[32] Page 90. "Le chrétien élevé a cet état (mystique) connait Dieu d'une façon quasi expérimentale, dans le pur miroir de la grace sanctifiante, don crée, mais tout divin, arrhes et aurore de la vie eternelle, qui révèle le Créateur sans se

confondre avec Lui. . . . Le néo-platonicien, le soufi, ne connait Dieu (en mettant les choses au mieux) que par une vue épurée de son ame". Grandmaison in a study of von Hügel cited by Père Lebreton in his *Life of Père de Grandmaison*, p. 201. The speculation suggested is whether the active denudation of the faculties demanded by St. John is not closely akin to the contemplative activity of natural mystics.

[33] Page 90. *The Cloud of Unknowing and other treatises*. With the commentary by Fr. Augustine Baker. Edited by Dom Justin McCann. (B.O.W.)

[34] Page 92. Cited by Bremond (*L'Histoire de la Spiritualité* from Marie de l'Incarnation by Charlevoix, p. 112.) See also *Le Témoignage de Marie de l'Incarnation*, edited by Dom Albert Jamet (Gabriel Beauchesne. Paris, 1932).

[35] Page 92. Poulain op. cit., chap. xviii, n. 40.

[26] Page 92. Poulain, chap. xvi, n. 25.

[37] Page 93. Brou, op. cit. gives a short summary of the development of Jesuit legislation concerning the hour's meditation.

[38] Page 93. Brou, op. cit., p. 19.

[39] Page 94. Nadal, Epist. t. 4, pp. 673-4.

[40] Page 105. Ecclus. xliii, 29.

[41] Page 113. Cf. Poulain, op. cit., chap. ix, nn. 18-23.

[42] Page 114. St. John, Dark Night: Cf. Abridgement ut supra, p. 109: "Those who are strong and able to bear suffering, are purified in more intense trials. But those who are weak are purified very slowly, with weak temptations, and the night of their purgation is long; their senses are refreshed from time to time lest they should fall away."

[43] Page 122. *Témoignage* ut supra (note 34), p. 31.

[44] Page 124. Ephesians i, 12.